C-1433   CAREER EXAMINATION SERIES

This is your
PASSBOOK for...

Project Manager

Test Preparation Study Guide
Questions & Answers

COPYRIGHT NOTICE

This book is SOLELY intended for, is sold ONLY to, and its use is RESTRICTED to individual, bona fide applicants or candidates who qualify by virtue of having seriously filed applications for appropriate license, certificate, professional and/or promotional advancement, higher school matriculation, scholarship, or other legitimate requirements of education and/or governmental authorities.

This book is NOT intended for use, class instruction, tutoring, training, duplication, copying, reprinting, excerption, or adaptation, etc., by:

1) Other publishers
2) Proprietors and/or Instructors of "Coaching" and/or Preparatory Courses
3) Personnel and/or Training Divisions of commercial, industrial, and governmental organizations
4) Schools, colleges, or universities and/or their departments and staffs, including teachers and other personnel
5) Testing Agencies or Bureaus
6) Study groups which seek by the purchase of a single volume to copy and/or duplicate and/or adapt this material for use by the group as a whole without having purchased individual volumes for each of the members of the group
7) Et al.

Such persons would be in violation of appropriate Federal and State statutes.

PROVISION OF LICENSING AGREEMENTS – Recognized educational, commercial, industrial, and governmental institutions and organizations, and others legitimately engaged in educational pursuits, including training, testing, and measurement activities, may address request for a licensing agreement to the copyright owners, who will determine whether, and under what conditions, including fees and charges, the materials in this book may be used them. In other words, a licensing facility exists for the legitimate use of the material in this book on other than an individual basis. However, it is asseverated and affirmed here that the material in this book CANNOT be used without the receipt of the express permission of such a licensing agreement from the Publishers. Inquiries re licensing should be addressed to the company, attention rights and permissions department.

All rights reserved, including the right of reproduction in whole or in part, in any form or by any means, electronic or mechanical, including photocopying, recording, or by any information storage and retrieval system, without permission in writing from the Publisher.

Copyright © 2024 by
National Learning Corporation

212 Michael Drive, Syosset, NY 11791
(516) 921-8888 • www.passbooks.com
E-mail: info@passbooks.com

PUBLISHED IN THE UNITED STATES OF AMERICA

PASSBOOK® SERIES

THE *PASSBOOK® SERIES* has been created to prepare applicants and candidates for the ultimate academic battlefield – the examination room.

At some time in our lives, each and every one of us may be required to take an examination – for validation, matriculation, admission, qualification, registration, certification, or licensure.

Based on the assumption that every applicant or candidate has met the basic formal educational standards, has taken the required number of courses, and read the necessary texts, the *PASSBOOK® SERIES* furnishes the one special preparation which may assure passing with confidence, instead of failing with insecurity. Examination questions – together with answers – are furnished as the basic vehicle for study so that the mysteries of the examination and its compounding difficulties may be eliminated or diminished by a sure method.

This book is meant to help you pass your examination provided that you qualify and are serious in your objective.

The entire field is reviewed through the huge store of content information which is succinctly presented through a provocative and challenging approach – the question-and-answer method.

A climate of success is established by furnishing the correct answers at the end of each test.

You soon learn to recognize types of questions, forms of questions, and patterns of questioning. You may even begin to anticipate expected outcomes.

You perceive that many questions are repeated or adapted so that you can gain acute insights, which may enable you to score many sure points.

You learn how to confront new questions, or types of questions, and to attack them confidently and work out the correct answers.

You note objectives and emphases, and recognize pitfalls and dangers, so that you may make positive educational adjustments.

Moreover, you are kept fully informed in relation to new concepts, methods, practices, and directions in the field.

You discover that you are actually taking the examination all the time: you are preparing for the examination by "taking" an examination, not by reading extraneous and/or supererogatory textbooks.

In short, this PASSBOOK®, used directedly, should be an important factor in helping you to pass your test.

PROJECT MANAGER

DUTIES:
Under the general supervision of a higher-level administrator, this position is responsible for the coordination and implementation of educational technology projects, which encompasses both administrative and/or instructional projects in the school district. The incumbent coordinates steps in the planning, ordering and installation, and follow-up service cycle, as well as work assignments of various personnel from different departments within the district, vendors, and/or consultants as necessary to complete the project. Supervision may be a responsibility of this position. Does related work as required.

SCOPE OF THE EXAMINATION:
The written test is designed to test for knowledge, skills, and/or abilities in such areas as:
1. **Project management** - These questions are designed to test for techniques and concepts of project management. They may cover, but not necessarily be confined to, management of systems development, management by objectives, project scheduling and control techniques (e.g., PERT), characteristics of organizations and of the systems life cycle, and the development of data processing standards.
2. **Administration** - These questions test for knowledge of the managerial functions involved in directing an organization or an organizational segment. These questions cover such areas as: developing objectives and formulating policies; making decisions based on the context of the administrator's position and authority; forecasting and planning; organizing; developing personnel; coordinating and informing; guiding and leading; testing and evaluating; and budgeting.
3. **Supervision** - These questions test for knowledge of the principles and practices employed in planning, organizing, and controlling the activities of a work unit toward predetermined objectives. The concepts covered, usually in a situational question format, include such topics as assigning and reviewing work; evaluating performance; maintaining work standards; motivating and developing subordinates; implementing procedural change; increasing efficiency; and dealing with problems of absenteeism, morale, and discipline.
4. **Preparing written material** - These questions test for the ability to present information clearly and accurately, and to organize paragraphs logically and comprehensibly. For some questions, you will be given information in two or three sentences followed by four restatements of the information. You must then choose the best version. For other questions, you will be given paragraphs with their sentences out of order. You must then choose, from four suggestions, the best order for the sentences.

HOW TO TAKE A TEST

I. YOU MUST PASS AN EXAMINATION

A. *WHAT EVERY CANDIDATE SHOULD KNOW*

Examination applicants often ask us for help in preparing for the written test. What can I study in advance? What kinds of questions will be asked? How will the test be given? How will the papers be graded?

As an applicant for a civil service examination, you may be wondering about some of these things. Our purpose here is to suggest effective methods of advance study and to describe civil service examinations.

Your chances for success on this examination can be increased if you know how to prepare. Those "pre-examination jitters" can be reduced if you know what to expect. You can even experience an adventure in good citizenship if you know why civil service exams are given.

B. *WHY ARE CIVIL SERVICE EXAMINATIONS GIVEN?*

Civil service examinations are important to you in two ways. As a citizen, you want public jobs filled by employees who know how to do their work. As a job seeker, you want a fair chance to compete for that job on an equal footing with other candidates. The best-known means of accomplishing this two-fold goal is the competitive examination.

Exams are widely publicized throughout the nation. They may be administered for jobs in federal, state, city, municipal, town or village governments or agencies.

Any citizen may apply, with some limitations, such as the age or residence of applicants. Your experience and education may be reviewed to see whether you meet the requirements for the particular examination. When these requirements exist, they are reasonable and applied consistently to all applicants. Thus, a competitive examination may cause you some uneasiness now, but it is your privilege and safeguard.

C. *HOW ARE CIVIL SERVICE EXAMS DEVELOPED?*

Examinations are carefully written by trained technicians who are specialists in the field known as "psychological measurement," in consultation with recognized authorities in the field of work that the test will cover. These experts recommend the subject matter areas or skills to be tested; only those knowledges or skills important to your success on the job are included. The most reliable books and source materials available are used as references. Together, the experts and technicians judge the difficulty level of the questions.

Test technicians know how to phrase questions so that the problem is clearly stated. Their ethics do not permit "trick" or "catch" questions. Questions may have been tried out on sample groups, or subjected to statistical analysis, to determine their usefulness.

Written tests are often used in combination with performance tests, ratings of training and experience, and oral interviews. All of these measures combine to form the best-known means of finding the right person for the right job.

II. HOW TO PASS THE WRITTEN TEST

A. NATURE OF THE EXAMINATION

To prepare intelligently for civil service examinations, you should know how they differ from school examinations you have taken. In school you were assigned certain definite pages to read or subjects to cover. The examination questions were quite detailed and usually emphasized memory. Civil service exams, on the other hand, try to discover your present ability to perform the duties of a position, plus your potentiality to learn these duties. In other words, a civil service exam attempts to predict how successful you will be. Questions cover such a broad area that they cannot be as minute and detailed as school exam questions.

In the public service similar kinds of work, or positions, are grouped together in one "class." This process is known as *position-classification*. All the positions in a class are paid according to the salary range for that class. One class title covers all of these positions, and they are all tested by the same examination.

B. FOUR BASIC STEPS

1) Study the announcement

How, then, can you know what subjects to study? Our best answer is: "Learn as much as possible about the class of positions for which you've applied." The exam will test the knowledge, skills and abilities needed to do the work.

Your most valuable source of information about the position you want is the official exam announcement. This announcement lists the training and experience qualifications. Check these standards and apply only if you come reasonably close to meeting them.

The brief description of the position in the examination announcement offers some clues to the subjects which will be tested. Think about the job itself. Review the duties in your mind. Can you perform them, or are there some in which you are rusty? Fill in the blank spots in your preparation.

Many jurisdictions preview the written test in the exam announcement by including a section called "Knowledge and Abilities Required," "Scope of the Examination," or some similar heading. Here you will find out specifically what fields will be tested.

2) Review your own background

Once you learn in general what the position is all about, and what you need to know to do the work, ask yourself which subjects you already know fairly well and which need improvement. You may wonder whether to concentrate on improving your strong areas or on building some background in your fields of weakness. When the announcement has specified "some knowledge" or "considerable knowledge," or has used adjectives like "beginning principles of…" or "advanced … methods," you can get a clue as to the number and difficulty of questions to be asked in any given field. More questions, and hence broader coverage, would be included for those subjects which are more important in the work. Now weigh your strengths and weaknesses against the job requirements and prepare accordingly.

3) Determine the level of the position

Another way to tell how intensively you should prepare is to understand the level of the job for which you are applying. Is it the entering level? In other words, is this the position in which beginners in a field of work are hired? Or is it an intermediate or advanced level? Sometimes this is indicated by such words as "Junior" or "Senior" in the class title. Other jurisdictions use Roman numerals to designate the level – Clerk I, Clerk II, for example. The word "Supervisor" sometimes appears in the title. If the level is not indicated by the title, check the description of duties. Will you be working under very close supervision, or will you have responsibility for independent decisions in this work?

4) Choose appropriate study materials

Now that you know the subjects to be examined and the relative amount of each subject to be covered, you can choose suitable study materials. For beginning level jobs, or even advanced ones, if you have a pronounced weakness in some aspect of your training, read a modern, standard textbook in that field. Be sure it is up to date and has general coverage. Such books are normally available at your library, and the librarian will be glad to help you locate one. For entry-level positions, questions of appropriate difficulty are chosen -- neither highly advanced questions, nor those too simple. Such questions require careful thought but not advanced training.

If the position for which you are applying is technical or advanced, you will read more advanced, specialized material. If you are already familiar with the basic principles of your field, elementary textbooks would waste your time. Concentrate on advanced textbooks and technical periodicals. Think through the concepts and review difficult problems in your field.

These are all general sources. You can get more ideas on your own initiative, following these leads. For example, training manuals and publications of the government agency which employs workers in your field can be useful, particularly for technical and professional positions. A letter or visit to the government department involved may result in more specific study suggestions, and certainly will provide you with a more definite idea of the exact nature of the position you are seeking.

III. KINDS OF TESTS

Tests are used for purposes other than measuring knowledge and ability to perform specified duties. For some positions, it is equally important to test ability to make adjustments to new situations or to profit from training. In others, basic mental abilities not dependent on information are essential. Questions which test these things may not appear as pertinent to the duties of the position as those which test for knowledge and information. Yet they are often highly important parts of a fair examination. For very general questions, it is almost impossible to help you direct your study efforts. What we can do is to point out some of the more common of these general abilities needed in public service positions and describe some typical questions.

1) General information

Broad, general information has been found useful for predicting job success in some kinds of work. This is tested in a variety of ways, from vocabulary lists to questions about current events. Basic background in some field of work, such as sociology or economics, may be sampled in a group of questions. Often these are principles which have become familiar to most persons through exposure rather than through formal training. It is difficult to advise you how to study for these questions; being alert to the world around you is our best suggestion.

2) Verbal ability

An example of an ability needed in many positions is verbal or language ability. Verbal ability is, in brief, the ability to use and understand words. Vocabulary and grammar tests are typical measures of this ability. Reading comprehension or paragraph interpretation questions are common in many kinds of civil service tests. You are given a paragraph of written material and asked to find its central meaning.

3) Numerical ability

Number skills can be tested by the familiar arithmetic problem, by checking paired lists of numbers to see which are alike and which are different, or by interpreting charts and graphs. In the latter test, a graph may be printed in the test booklet which you are asked to use as the basis for answering questions.

4) Observation

A popular test for law-enforcement positions is the observation test. A picture is shown to you for several minutes, then taken away. Questions about the picture test your ability to observe both details and larger elements.

5) Following directions

In many positions in the public service, the employee must be able to carry out written instructions dependably and accurately. You may be given a chart with several columns, each column listing a variety of information. The questions require you to carry out directions involving the information given in the chart.

6) Skills and aptitudes

Performance tests effectively measure some manual skills and aptitudes. When the skill is one in which you are trained, such as typing or shorthand, you can practice. These tests are often very much like those given in business school or high school courses. For many of the other skills and aptitudes, however, no short-time preparation can be made. Skills and abilities natural to you or that you have developed throughout your lifetime are being tested.

Many of the general questions just described provide all the data needed to answer the questions and ask you to use your reasoning ability to find the answers. Your best preparation for these tests, as well as for tests of facts and ideas, is to be at your physical and mental best. You, no doubt, have your own methods of getting into an exam-taking mood and keeping "in shape." The next section lists some ideas on this subject.

IV. KINDS OF QUESTIONS

Only rarely is the "essay" question, which you answer in narrative form, used in civil service tests. Civil service tests are usually of the short-answer type. Full instructions for answering these questions will be given to you at the examination. But in case this is your first experience with short-answer questions and separate answer sheets, here is what you need to know:

1) Multiple-choice Questions

Most popular of the short-answer questions is the "multiple choice" or "best answer" question. It can be used, for example, to test for factual knowledge, ability to solve problems or judgment in meeting situations found at work.

A multiple-choice question is normally one of three types—
- It can begin with an incomplete statement followed by several possible endings. You are to find the one ending which *best* completes the statement, although some of the others may not be entirely wrong.
- It can also be a complete statement in the form of a question which is answered by choosing one of the statements listed.

- It can be in the form of a problem – again you select the best answer.

Here is an example of a multiple-choice question with a discussion which should give you some clues as to the method for choosing the right answer:

When an employee has a complaint about his assignment, the action which will *best* help him overcome his difficulty is to
  A. discuss his difficulty with his coworkers
  B. take the problem to the head of the organization
  C. take the problem to the person who gave him the assignment
  D. say nothing to anyone about his complaint

In answering this question, you should study each of the choices to find which is best. Consider choice "A" – Certainly an employee may discuss his complaint with fellow employees, but no change or improvement can result, and the complaint remains unresolved. Choice "B" is a poor choice since the head of the organization probably does not know what assignment you have been given, and taking your problem to him is known as "going over the head" of the supervisor. The supervisor, or person who made the assignment, is the person who can clarify it or correct any injustice. Choice "C" is, therefore, correct. To say nothing, as in choice "D," is unwise. Supervisors have and interest in knowing the problems employees are facing, and the employee is seeking a solution to his problem.

2) True/False Questions

The "true/false" or "right/wrong" form of question is sometimes used. Here a complete statement is given. Your job is to decide whether the statement is right or wrong.

SAMPLE: A roaming cell-phone call to a nearby city costs less than a non-roaming call to a distant city.

This statement is wrong, or false, since roaming calls are more expensive.

This is not a complete list of all possible question forms, although most of the others are variations of these common types. You will always get complete directions for answering questions. Be sure you understand *how* to mark your answers – ask questions until you do.

V. RECORDING YOUR ANSWERS

Computer terminals are used more and more today for many different kinds of exams.
For an examination with very few applicants, you may be told to record your answers in the test booklet itself. Separate answer sheets are much more common. If this separate answer sheet is to be scored by machine – and this is often the case – it is highly important that you mark your answers correctly in order to get credit.

An electronic scoring machine is often used in civil service offices because of the speed with which papers can be scored. Machine-scored answer sheets must be marked with a pencil, which will be given to you. This pencil has a high graphite content which responds to the electronic scoring machine. As a matter of fact, stray dots may register as answers, so do not let your pencil rest on the answer sheet while you are pondering the correct answer. Also, if your pencil lead breaks or is otherwise defective, ask for another.

Since the answer sheet will be dropped in a slot in the scoring machine, be careful not to bend the corners or get the paper crumpled.

The answer sheet normally has five vertical columns of numbers, with 30 numbers to a column. These numbers correspond to the question numbers in your test booklet. After each number, going across the page are four or five pairs of dotted lines. These short dotted lines have small letters or numbers above them. The first two pairs may also have a "T" or "F" above the letters. This indicates that the first two pairs only are to be used if the questions are of the true-false type. If the questions are multiple choice, disregard the "T" and "F" and pay attention only to the small letters or numbers.

Answer your questions in the manner of the sample that follows:

32. The largest city in the United States is
    A. Washington, D.C.
    B. New York City
    C. Chicago
    D. Detroit
    E. San Francisco

1) Choose the answer you think is best. (New York City is the largest, so "B" is correct.)
2) Find the row of dotted lines numbered the same as the question you are answering. (Find row number 32)
3) Find the pair of dotted lines corresponding to the answer. (Find the pair of lines under the mark "B.")
4) Make a solid black mark between the dotted lines.

VI. BEFORE THE TEST

Common sense will help you find procedures to follow to get ready for an examination. Too many of us, however, overlook these sensible measures. Indeed, nervousness and fatigue have been found to be the most serious reasons why applicants fail to do their best on civil service tests. Here is a list of reminders:

- Begin your preparation early – Don't wait until the last minute to go scurrying around for books and materials or to find out what the position is all about.
- Prepare continuously – An hour a night for a week is better than an all-night cram session. This has been definitely established. What is more, a night a week for a month will return better dividends than crowding your study into a shorter period of time.
- Locate the place of the exam – You have been sent a notice telling you when and where to report for the examination. If the location is in a different town or otherwise unfamiliar to you, it would be well to inquire the best route and learn something about the building.
- Relax the night before the test – Allow your mind to rest. Do not study at all that night. Plan some mild recreation or diversion; then go to bed early and get a good night's sleep.
- Get up early enough to make a leisurely trip to the place for the test – This way unforeseen events, traffic snarls, unfamiliar buildings, etc. will not upset you.
- Dress comfortably – A written test is not a fashion show. You will be known by number and not by name, so wear something comfortable.

- Leave excess paraphernalia at home – Shopping bags and odd bundles will get in your way. You need bring only the items mentioned in the official notice you received; usually everything you need is provided. Do not bring reference books to the exam. They will only confuse those last minutes and be taken away from you when in the test room.
- Arrive somewhat ahead of time – If because of transportation schedules you must get there very early, bring a newspaper or magazine to take your mind off yourself while waiting.
- Locate the examination room – When you have found the proper room, you will be directed to the seat or part of the room where you will sit. Sometimes you are given a sheet of instructions to read while you are waiting. Do not fill out any forms until you are told to do so; just read them and be prepared.
- Relax and prepare to listen to the instructions
- If you have any physical problem that may keep you from doing your best, be sure to tell the test administrator. If you are sick or in poor health, you really cannot do your best on the exam. You can come back and take the test some other time.

VII. AT THE TEST

The day of the test is here and you have the test booklet in your hand. The temptation to get going is very strong. Caution! There is more to success than knowing the right answers. You must know how to identify your papers and understand variations in the type of short-answer question used in this particular examination. Follow these suggestions for maximum results from your efforts:

1) Cooperate with the monitor

The test administrator has a duty to create a situation in which you can be as much at ease as possible. He will give instructions, tell you when to begin, check to see that you are marking your answer sheet correctly, and so on. He is not there to guard you, although he will see that your competitors do not take unfair advantage. He wants to help you do your best.

2) Listen to all instructions

Don't jump the gun! Wait until you understand all directions. In most civil service tests you get more time than you need to answer the questions. So don't be in a hurry. Read each word of instructions until you clearly understand the meaning. Study the examples, listen to all announcements and follow directions. Ask questions if you do not understand what to do.

3) Identify your papers

Civil service exams are usually identified by number only. You will be assigned a number; you must not put your name on your test papers. Be sure to copy your number correctly. Since more than one exam may be given, copy your exact examination title.

4) Plan your time

Unless you are told that a test is a "speed" or "rate of work" test, speed itself is usually not important. Time enough to answer all the questions will be provided, but this does not mean that you have all day. An overall time limit has been set. Divide the total time (in minutes) by the number of questions to determine the approximate time you have for each question.

5) Do not linger over difficult questions

If you come across a difficult question, mark it with a paper clip (useful to have along) and come back to it when you have been through the booklet. One caution if you do this – be sure to skip a number on your answer sheet as well. Check often to be sure that you have not lost your place and that you are marking in the row numbered the same as the question you are answering.

6) Read the questions

Be sure you know what the question asks! Many capable people are unsuccessful because they failed to *read* the questions correctly.

7) Answer all questions

Unless you have been instructed that a penalty will be deducted for incorrect answers, it is better to guess than to omit a question.

8) Speed tests

It is often better NOT to guess on speed tests. It has been found that on timed tests people are tempted to spend the last few seconds before time is called in marking answers at random – without even reading them – in the hope of picking up a few extra points. To discourage this practice, the instructions may warn you that your score will be "corrected" for guessing. That is, a penalty will be applied. The incorrect answers will be deducted from the correct ones, or some other penalty formula will be used.

9) Review your answers

If you finish before time is called, go back to the questions you guessed or omitted to give them further thought. Review other answers if you have time.

10) Return your test materials

If you are ready to leave before others have finished or time is called, take ALL your materials to the monitor and leave quietly. Never take any test material with you. The monitor can discover whose papers are not complete, and taking a test booklet may be grounds for disqualification.

VIII. EXAMINATION TECHNIQUES

1) Read the general instructions carefully. These are usually printed on the first page of the exam booklet. As a rule, these instructions refer to the timing of the examination; the fact that you should not start work until the signal and must stop work at a signal, etc. If there are any *special* instructions, such as a choice of questions to be answered, make sure that you note this instruction carefully.

2) When you are ready to start work on the examination, that is as soon as the signal has been given, read the instructions to each question booklet, underline any key words or phrases, such as *least, best, outline, describe* and the like. In this way you will tend to answer as requested rather than discover on reviewing your paper that you *listed without describing*, that you selected the *worst* choice rather than the *best* choice, etc.

3) If the examination is of the objective or multiple-choice type – that is, each question will also give a series of possible answers: A, B, C or D, and you are called upon to select the best answer and write the letter next to that answer on your answer paper – it is advisable to start answering each question in turn. There may be anywhere from 50 to 100 such questions in the three or four hours allotted and you can see how much time would be taken if you read through all the questions before beginning to answer any. Furthermore, if you come across a question or group of questions which you know would be difficult to answer, it would undoubtedly affect your handling of all the other questions.

4) If the examination is of the essay type and contains but a few questions, it is a moot point as to whether you should read all the questions before starting to answer any one. Of course, if you are given a choice – say five out of seven and the like – then it is essential to read all the questions so you can eliminate the two that are most difficult. If, however, you are asked to answer all the questions, there may be danger in trying to answer the easiest one first because you may find that you will spend too much time on it. The best technique is to answer the first question, then proceed to the second, etc.

5) Time your answers. Before the exam begins, write down the time it started, then add the time allowed for the examination and write down the time it must be completed, then divide the time available somewhat as follows:
    - If 3-1/2 hours are allowed, that would be 210 minutes. If you have 80 objective-type questions, that would be an average of 2-1/2 minutes per question. Allow yourself no more than 2 minutes per question, or a total of 160 minutes, which will permit about 50 minutes to review.
    - If for the time allotment of 210 minutes there are 7 essay questions to answer, that would average about 30 minutes a question. Give yourself only 25 minutes per question so that you have about 35 minutes to review.

6) The most important instruction is to *read each question* and make sure you know what is wanted. The second most important instruction is to *time yourself properly* so that you answer every question. The third most important instruction is to *answer every question*. Guess if you have to but include something for each question. Remember that you will receive no credit for a blank and will probably receive some credit if you write something in answer to an essay question. If you guess a letter – say "B" for a multiple-choice question – you may have guessed right. If you leave a blank as an answer to a multiple-choice question, the examiners may respect your feelings but it will not add a point to your score. Some exams may penalize you for wrong answers, so in such cases *only*, you may not want to guess unless you have some basis for your answer.

7) Suggestions
    a. Objective-type questions
        1. Examine the question booklet for proper sequence of pages and questions
        2. Read all instructions carefully
        3. Skip any question which seems too difficult; return to it after all other questions have been answered
        4. Apportion your time properly; do not spend too much time on any single question or group of questions

5. Note and underline key words – *all, most, fewest, least, best, worst, same, opposite,* etc.
6. Pay particular attention to negatives
7. Note unusual option, e.g., unduly long, short, complex, different or similar in content to the body of the question
8. Observe the use of "hedging" words – *probably, may, most likely,* etc.
9. Make sure that your answer is put next to the same number as the question
10. Do not second-guess unless you have good reason to believe the second answer is definitely more correct
11. Cross out original answer if you decide another answer is more accurate; do not erase until you are ready to hand your paper in
12. Answer all questions; guess unless instructed otherwise
13. Leave time for review

  b. Essay questions
   1. Read each question carefully
   2. Determine exactly what is wanted. Underline key words or phrases.
   3. Decide on outline or paragraph answer
   4. Include many different points and elements unless asked to develop any one or two points or elements
   5. Show impartiality by giving pros and cons unless directed to select one side only
   6. Make and write down any assumptions you find necessary to answer the questions
   7. Watch your English, grammar, punctuation and choice of words
   8. Time your answers; don't crowd material

8) Answering the essay question

Most essay questions can be answered by framing the specific response around several key words or ideas. Here are a few such key words or ideas:

M's: manpower, materials, methods, money, management
P's: purpose, program, policy, plan, procedure, practice, problems, pitfalls, personnel, public relations
  a. Six basic steps in handling problems:
   1. Preliminary plan and background development
   2. Collect information, data and facts
   3. Analyze and interpret information, data and facts
   4. Analyze and develop solutions as well as make recommendations
   5. Prepare report and sell recommendations
   6. Install recommendations and follow up effectiveness

  b. Pitfalls to avoid
   1. *Taking things for granted* – A statement of the situation does not necessarily imply that each of the elements is necessarily true; for example, a complaint may be invalid and biased so that all that can be taken for granted is that a complaint has been registered

2. *Considering only one side of a situation* – Wherever possible, indicate several alternatives and then point out the reasons you selected the best one
3. *Failing to indicate follow up* – Whenever your answer indicates action on your part, make certain that you will take proper follow-up action to see how successful your recommendations, procedures or actions turn out to be
4. *Taking too long in answering any single question* – Remember to time your answers properly

IX. AFTER THE TEST

Scoring procedures differ in detail among civil service jurisdictions although the general principles are the same. Whether the papers are hand-scored or graded by machine we have described, they are nearly always graded by number. That is, the person who marks the paper knows only the number – never the name – of the applicant. Not until all the papers have been graded will they be matched with names. If other tests, such as training and experience or oral interview ratings have been given, scores will be combined. Different parts of the examination usually have different weights. For example, the written test might count 60 percent of the final grade, and a rating of training and experience 40 percent. In many jurisdictions, veterans will have a certain number of points added to their grades.

After the final grade has been determined, the names are placed in grade order and an eligible list is established. There are various methods for resolving ties between those who get the same final grade – probably the most common is to place first the name of the person whose application was received first. Job offers are made from the eligible list in the order the names appear on it. You will be notified of your grade and your rank as soon as all these computations have been made. This will be done as rapidly as possible.

People who are found to meet the requirements in the announcement are called "eligibles." Their names are put on a list of eligible candidates. An eligible's chances of getting a job depend on how high he stands on this list and how fast agencies are filling jobs from the list.

When a job is to be filled from a list of eligibles, the agency asks for the names of people on the list of eligibles for that job. When the civil service commission receives this request, it sends to the agency the names of the three people highest on this list. Or, if the job to be filled has specialized requirements, the office sends the agency the names of the top three persons who meet these requirements from the general list.

The appointing officer makes a choice from among the three people whose names were sent to him. If the selected person accepts the appointment, the names of the others are put back on the list to be considered for future openings.

That is the rule in hiring from all kinds of eligible lists, whether they are for typist, carpenter, chemist, or something else. For every vacancy, the appointing officer has his choice of any one of the top three eligibles on the list. This explains why the person whose name is on top of the list sometimes does not get an appointment when some of the persons lower on the list do. If the appointing officer chooses the second or third eligible, the No. 1 eligible does not get a job at once, but stays on the list until he is appointed or the list is terminated.

X. HOW TO PASS THE INTERVIEW TEST

The examination for which you applied requires an oral interview test. You have already taken the written test and you are now being called for the interview test – the final part of the formal examination.

You may think that it is not possible to prepare for an interview test and that there are no procedures to follow during an interview. Our purpose is to point out some things you can do in advance that will help you and some good rules to follow and pitfalls to avoid while you are being interviewed.

What is an interview supposed to test?

The written examination is designed to test the technical knowledge and competence of the candidate; the oral is designed to evaluate intangible qualities, not readily measured otherwise, and to establish a list showing the relative fitness of each candidate – as measured against his competitors – for the position sought. Scoring is not on the basis of "right" and "wrong," but on a sliding scale of values ranging from "not passable" to "outstanding." As a matter of fact, it is possible to achieve a relatively low score without a single "incorrect" answer because of evident weakness in the qualities being measured.

Occasionally, an examination may consist entirely of an oral test – either an individual or a group oral. In such cases, information is sought concerning the technical knowledges and abilities of the candidate, since there has been no written examination for this purpose. More commonly, however, an oral test is used to supplement a written examination.

Who conducts interviews?

The composition of oral boards varies among different jurisdictions. In nearly all, a representative of the personnel department serves as chairman. One of the members of the board may be a representative of the department in which the candidate would work. In some cases, "outside experts" are used, and, frequently, a businessman or some other representative of the general public is asked to serve. Labor and management or other special groups may be represented. The aim is to secure the services of experts in the appropriate field.

However the board is composed, it is a good idea (and not at all improper or unethical) to ascertain in advance of the interview who the members are and what groups they represent. When you are introduced to them, you will have some idea of their backgrounds and interests, and at least you will not stutter and stammer over their names.

What should be done before the interview?

While knowledge about the board members is useful and takes some of the surprise element out of the interview, there is other preparation which is more substantive. It *is* possible to prepare for an oral interview – in several ways:

1) Keep a copy of your application and review it carefully before the interview

This may be the only document before the oral board, and the starting point of the interview. Know what education and experience you have listed there, and the sequence and dates of all of it. Sometimes the board will ask you to review the highlights of your experience for them; you should not have to hem and haw doing it.

2) Study the class specification and the examination announcement

Usually, the oral board has one or both of these to guide them. The qualities, characteristics or knowledges required by the position sought are stated in these documents. They offer valuable clues as to the nature of the oral interview. For example, if the job involves supervisory responsibilities, the announcement will usually indicate that knowledge of modern supervisory methods and the qualifications of the candidate as a supervisor will be tested. If so, you can expect such questions, frequently in the form of a hypothetical situation which you are expected to solve. NEVER go into an oral without knowledge of the duties and responsibilities of the job you seek.

3) Think through each qualification required

Try to visualize the kind of questions you would ask if you were a board member. How well could you answer them? Try especially to appraise your own knowledge and background in each area, *measured against the job sought*, and identify any areas in which you are weak. Be critical and realistic – do not flatter yourself.

4) Do some general reading in areas in which you feel you may be weak

For example, if the job involves supervision and your past experience has NOT, some general reading in supervisory methods and practices, particularly in the field of human relations, might be useful. Do NOT study agency procedures or detailed manuals. The oral board will be testing your understanding and capacity, not your memory.

5) Get a good night's sleep and watch your general health and mental attitude

You will want a clear head at the interview. Take care of a cold or any other minor ailment, and of course, no hangovers.

What should be done on the day of the interview?

Now comes the day of the interview itself. Give yourself plenty of time to get there. Plan to arrive somewhat ahead of the scheduled time, particularly if your appointment is in the fore part of the day. If a previous candidate fails to appear, the board might be ready for you a bit early. By early afternoon an oral board is almost invariably behind schedule if there are many candidates, and you may have to wait. Take along a book or magazine to read, or your application to review, but leave any extraneous material in the waiting room when you go in for your interview. In any event, relax and compose yourself.

The matter of dress is important. The board is forming impressions about you – from your experience, your manners, your attitude, and your appearance. Give your personal appearance careful attention. Dress your best, but not your flashiest. Choose conservative, appropriate clothing, and be sure it is immaculate. This is a business interview, and your appearance should indicate that you regard it as such. Besides, being well groomed and properly dressed will help boost your confidence.

Sooner or later, someone will call your name and escort you into the interview room. *This is it.* From here on you are on your own. It is too late for any more preparation. But remember, you asked for this opportunity to prove your fitness, and you are here because your request was granted.

What happens when you go in?

The usual sequence of events will be as follows: The clerk (who is often the board stenographer) will introduce you to the chairman of the oral board, who will introduce you to the other members of the board. Acknowledge the introductions before you sit down. Do not be surprised if you find a microphone facing you or a stenotypist sitting by. Oral interviews are usually recorded in the event of an appeal or other review.

Usually the chairman of the board will open the interview by reviewing the highlights of your education and work experience from your application – primarily for the benefit of the other members of the board, as well as to get the material into the record. Do not interrupt or comment unless there is an error or significant misinterpretation; if that is the case, do not hesitate. But do not quibble about insignificant matters. Also, he will usually ask you some question about your education, experience or your present job – partly to get you to start talking and to establish the interviewing "rapport." He may start the actual questioning, or turn it over to one of the other members. Frequently, each member undertakes the questioning on a particular area, one in which he is perhaps most competent, so you can expect each member to participate in the examination. Because time is limited, you may also expect some rather abrupt switches in the direction the questioning takes, so do not be upset by it. Normally, a board member will not pursue a single line of questioning unless he discovers a particular strength or weakness.

After each member has participated, the chairman will usually ask whether any member has any further questions, then will ask you if you have anything you wish to add. Unless you are expecting this question, it may floor you. Worse, it may start you off on an extended, extemporaneous speech. The board is not usually seeking more information. The question is principally to offer you a last opportunity to present further qualifications or to indicate that you have nothing to add. So, if you feel that a significant qualification or characteristic has been overlooked, it is proper to point it out in a sentence or so. Do not compliment the board on the thoroughness of their examination – they have been sketchy, and you know it. If you wish, merely say, "No thank you, I have nothing further to add." This is a point where you can "talk yourself out" of a good impression or fail to present an important bit of information. Remember, *you close the interview yourself.*

The chairman will then say, "That is all, Mr. _____, thank you." Do not be startled; the interview is over, and quicker than you think. Thank him, gather your belongings and take your leave. Save your sigh of relief for the other side of the door.

How to put your best foot forward

Throughout this entire process, you may feel that the board individually and collectively is trying to pierce your defenses, seek out your hidden weaknesses and embarrass and confuse you. Actually, this is not true. They are obliged to make an appraisal of your qualifications for the job you are seeking, and they want to see you in your best light. Remember, they must interview all candidates and a non-cooperative candidate may become a failure in spite of their best efforts to bring out his qualifications. Here are 15 suggestions that will help you:

1) **Be natural – Keep your attitude confident, not cocky**

If you are not confident that you can do the job, do not expect the board to be. Do not apologize for your weaknesses, try to bring out your strong points. The board is interested in a positive, not negative, presentation. Cockiness will antagonize any board member and make him wonder if you are covering up a weakness by a false show of strength.

2) **Get comfortable, but don't lounge or sprawl**

Sit erectly but not stiffly. A careless posture may lead the board to conclude that you are careless in other things, or at least that you are not impressed by the importance of the occasion. Either conclusion is natural, even if incorrect. Do not fuss with your clothing, a pencil or an ashtray. Your hands may occasionally be useful to emphasize a point; do not let them become a point of distraction.

3) **Do not wisecrack or make small talk**

This is a serious situation, and your attitude should show that you consider it as such. Further, the time of the board is limited – they do not want to waste it, and neither should you.

4) Do not exaggerate your experience or abilities
   In the first place, from information in the application or other interviews and sources, the board may know more about you than you think. Secondly, you probably will not get away with it. An experienced board is rather adept at spotting such a situation, so do not take the chance.

5) If you know a board member, do not make a point of it, yet do not hide it
   Certainly you are not fooling him, and probably not the other members of the board. Do not try to take advantage of your acquaintanceship – it will probably do you little good.

6) Do not dominate the interview
   Let the board do that. They will give you the clues – do not assume that you have to do all the talking. Realize that the board has a number of questions to ask you, and do not try to take up all the interview time by showing off your extensive knowledge of the answer to the first one.

7) Be attentive
   You only have 20 minutes or so, and you should keep your attention at its sharpest throughout. When a member is addressing a problem or question to you, give him your undivided attention. Address your reply principally to him, but do not exclude the other board members.

8) Do not interrupt
   A board member may be stating a problem for you to analyze. He will ask you a question when the time comes. Let him state the problem, and wait for the question.

9) Make sure you understand the question
   Do not try to answer until you are sure what the question is. If it is not clear, restate it in your own words or ask the board member to clarify it for you. However, do not haggle about minor elements.

10) Reply promptly but not hastily
   A common entry on oral board rating sheets is "candidate responded readily," or "candidate hesitated in replies." Respond as promptly and quickly as you can, but do not jump to a hasty, ill-considered answer.

11) Do not be peremptory in your answers
   A brief answer is proper – but do not fire your answer back. That is a losing game from your point of view. The board member can probably ask questions much faster than you can answer them.

12) Do not try to create the answer you think the board member wants
   He is interested in what kind of mind you have and how it works – not in playing games. Furthermore, he can usually spot this practice and will actually grade you down on it.

13) Do not switch sides in your reply merely to agree with a board member
   Frequently, a member will take a contrary position merely to draw you out and to see if you are willing and able to defend your point of view. Do not start a debate, yet do not surrender a good position. If a position is worth taking, it is worth defending.

14) Do not be afraid to admit an error in judgment if you are shown to be wrong

The board knows that you are forced to reply without any opportunity for careful consideration. Your answer may be demonstrably wrong. If so, admit it and get on with the interview.

15) Do not dwell at length on your present job

The opening question may relate to your present assignment. Answer the question but do not go into an extended discussion. You are being examined for a *new* job, not your present one. As a matter of fact, try to phrase ALL your answers in terms of the job for which you are being examined.

Basis of Rating

Probably you will forget most of these "do's" and "don'ts" when you walk into the oral interview room. Even remembering them all will not ensure you a passing grade. Perhaps you did not have the qualifications in the first place. But remembering them will help you to put your best foot forward, without treading on the toes of the board members.

Rumor and popular opinion to the contrary notwithstanding, an oral board wants you to make the best appearance possible. They know you are under pressure – but they also want to see how you respond to it as a guide to what your reaction would be under the pressures of the job you seek. They will be influenced by the degree of poise you display, the personal traits you show and the manner in which you respond.

ABOUT THIS BOOK

This book contains tests divided into Examination Sections. Go through each test, answering every question in the margin. We have also attached a sample answer sheet at the back of the book that can be removed and used. At the end of each test look at the answer key and check your answers. On the ones you got wrong, look at the right answer choice and learn. Do not fill in the answers first. Do not memorize the questions and answers, but understand the answer and principles involved. On your test, the questions will likely be different from the samples. Questions are changed and new ones added. If you understand these past questions you should have success with any changes that arise. Tests may consist of several types of questions. We have additional books on each subject should more study be advisable or necessary for you. Finally, the more you study, the better prepared you will be. This book is intended to be the last thing you study before you walk into the examination room. Prior study of relevant texts is also recommended. NLC publishes some of these in our Fundamental Series. Knowledge and good sense are important factors in passing your exam. Good luck also helps. So now study this Passbook, absorb the material contained within and take that knowledge into the examination. Then do your best to pass that exam.

EXAMINATION SECTION

SAMPLE TEST

PRINCIPLES AND PRACTICES OF PROGRAM PLANNING AND PROJECT MANAGEMENT

Test material will be presented in a multiple-choice question format.

Test Task: You will be presented with situations in which you must apply knowledge of program planning and project management in order to answer the questions correctly.

SAMPLE QUESTION:
Which one of the following is developed by the project manager to clearly define the boundaries of a project by detailing the product, deliverables, and major objectives?

- A. cost baseline
- B. scope statement
- C. risk management plan
- D. quality management plan

The correct answer to this sample question is Choice B.

Solution:

Choice A is not correct. A cost baseline is a time-phased budget that a project manager prepares to monitor and measure cost performance throughout the project life cycle. It does not define the product, deliverables, or major objectives of the project.

Choice B is the correct answer to this question. The scope statement is developed by the project manager to define the project boundaries by outlining the product, deliverables, and major objectives.

Choice C is not correct. A risk management plan is a document that a project manager prepares to foresee risks, estimate impacts, and define responses to issues. It does not define the product, deliverables, or major objectives of the project.

Choice D is not correct. A quality management plan is a document that a project manager prepares to define the acceptable level of quality, which is typically defined by the customer, and to describe how the project will ensure this level of quality in its deliverables and work processes. It does not define the product, deliverables, or major objectives of the project.

EXAMINATION SECTION
TEST 1

DIRECTIONS: Each question or incomplete statement is followed by several suggested answers or completions. Select the one that BEST answers the question or completes the statement. *PRINT THE LETTER OF THE CORRECT ANSWER IN THE SPACE AT THE RIGHT.*

1. _____ is commonly used to report on project performance.
    A. Earned Value Management
    B. WBS
    C. Quality Management Plan
    D. RBS

2. Which of the following is NOT a process associated with communications management?
    A. Distribute information
    B. Manage stakeholder expectations
    C. Plan communication
    D. Survey questionnaire

3. As a project manager, you are expected to make relevant information available to project stakeholders as planned. Which process does this relate to?
    A. Distribute information
    B. Manage stakeholder expectations
    C. Plan communication
    D. Report performance

4. Report performance involves all of the following EXCEPT
    A. collecting and distributing performance data
    B. collecting and distributing progress measurements
    C. collecting stakeholder information needs
    D. collecting and distributing forecasts

5. Of the following examples listed, which is a sign of feedback from the receiver?
    A. No written response from the receiver
    B. An acknowledgement or additional questions from the receiver
    C. Encoding the message by the receiver
    D. Decoding the message by the receiver

6. As a project manager you are expected to create a scope statement. Once you have the statement, you find it to be useful in all the following ways EXCEPT
    A. describing the purpose of the project
    B. describing the objectives of the project
    C. distributing information
    D. explaining the business problems the project is expected to solve

7. What are project deliverables?
   A. Tangible products that the project is expected to deliver
   B. Prioritized list of deliverables
   C. Project scope statement
   D. Project documents

8. As a project manager, you are arranging criteria for project completion criteria. You could organize it using all of the following EXCEPT
   A. functional department
   B. milestones
   C. tasks of projects
   D. project phase

9. Which of the following is not a task under "Developing human resource plan"?
   A. Documenting organizational relationships
   B. Looking for the availability of required human resources
   C. Identification and documentation of project roles and responsibilities
   D. Creating a staffing plan

10. If you are a project manager who is keen in managing a project team, you would undertake any of the following EXCEPT
    A. creating a staffing plan
    B. evaluating individual team member performance
    C. providing feedback
    D. resolving conflicts

11. Nurturing the team is a vital role of a project manager. If you have to do so, what would you avoid?
    A. Guide the team members as required
    B. Provide mentoring throughout the project
    C. Remove the team member who is found to be less skilled
    D. On-the-job training

12. War room creation is an example of
    A. co-location
    B. management skills
    C. rewards and recognitions
    D. establishing ground rules

13. The team member roles and responsibilities could be documented using all of the following EXCEPT
    A. functional chart
    B. text-oriented format
    C. hierarchical type organizational chart
    D. matrix-based responsibility chart

14. _____ is NOT an example of constraints placed upon the project by current organizational policies.
    A. Hiring freeze
    B. Reduced training funds
    C. Organizational chart templates
    D. Rewards and Increments Freeze

15. As a project manager, you have decided to have a virtual team. What kind of limitation would this create with regards to team development?
    A. Rewards and recognition
    B. Establishing ground rules
    C. Team building
    D. Co-location

16. Unplanned training means
    A. team building using virtual team arrangement
    B. competencies developed as a result of project performance appraisals
    C. on-the-job training
    D. training that is done without any planning in advance

17. Resource break down structure is an example of
    A. functional chart
    B. text-oriented format
    C. hierarchical type organizational chart
    D. matrix-based responsibility chart

18. A project manager would consider the following as inputs to define scope EXCEPT
    A. requirements document
    B. project Charter
    C. product management plan
    D. organizational process charts

19. Aldo is a project manager and has to terminate a project earlier than planned. The level and extent of completion should be documented. Under which is this done?
    A. Verify scope
    B. Create scope
    C. Control scope
    D. Define scope

20. Sam, an IT project manager, is having difficulty in getting resources for his project, and hence has to depend highly on department heads. Which type of organization is Sam most likely working with?
    A. Functional
    B. Tight matrix
    C. Weak matrix
    D. Projectized

Questions 21-25.

Len is a project manager of an infrastructure project manager of a well-known company. He is involved in various processes of scope management. Look at the following chart and align the different processes to various tasks listed. Choose the appropriate answer for each process and list them under corresponding tasks.

	Processes	Corresponding tasks	List of tasks
21.	Define scope	21._____	A. Monitoring project scope and project status
22.	Control scope	22._____	B. Defining and documenting stakeholder needs
23.	Collect requirements	23._____	C. Formalizing acceptance of the complete project deliverables
24.	Verify scope	24._____	D. Breaking down the project into smaller, more manageable tasks
25.	Create WBS	25._____	E. Developing a detailed description of the project and its ultimate product

---

KEY (CORRECT ANSWERS)

1. A
2. D
3. A
4. C
5. B

6. C
7. A
8. C
9. B
10. A

11. C
12. A
13. A
14. C
15. D

16. B
17. C
18. C
19. A
20. A

21. E
22. A
23. B
24. C
25. D

TEST 2

DIRECTIONS: Each question or incomplete statement is followed by several suggested answers or completions. Select the one that BEST answers the question or completes the statement. *PRINT THE LETTER OF THE CORRECT ANSWER IN THE SPACE AT THE RIGHT.*

1. In which of the following processes would risk be identified? 1._____
   A. Risk identification
   B. Risk monitoring and control
   C. Qualitative risk analysis
   D. Risk identification, monitoring and control

2. Jack has prepared a risk management plan for his project and also identified risks in his project. Which of the following processes should Jack do next? 2._____
   A. Plan risk responses
   B. Perform qualitative analysis
   C. Perform quantitative analysis
   D. Monitor and control risk

3. Which of the following is NOT a step in risk management? 3._____
   A. Perform qualitative analysis
   B. Monitor and control risk
   C. Risk identification
   D. Risk breakdown structure

4. Sue is a project manager for an IT project at a corporate office. She is engaged in the process of identifying risks. To do so, she collects inputs from experts from the field through a questionnaire. What is this technique called? 4._____
   A. Interview
   B. Documentation review
   C. Delphi technique
   D. Register risk

5. Positive risks may be responded by which of the following: 5._____
   I. Exploit II. Accept III. Mitigate IV. Share

   A. I and III
   B. All of the above
   C. I, II and IV
   D. I, II and III

6. Risk _____ is a response to negative risks. 6._____
   A. identification
   B. mitigation
   C. response plan
   D. management plan

7

7. Which of the following statements is NOT true about risk management?
   A. Risk register documents all the risks in detail
   B. Risks always have negative impacts and not positive
   C. Risk mitigation is a response to negative risks
   D. Risk register documents the risks in detail

8. _____ is the document that lists all the risks in a hierarchical fashion.
   A. Risk breakdown structure
   B. Lists of risks
   C. Risk management plan
   D. Monte Carlo diagram

9. Nicole is a project manager of a reforestation project. In one of the project reviews, she realizes that a risk has occurred. Which document should Nicole refer to take an appropriate action?
   A. Risk response plan
   B. Risk register
   C. Risk management plan
   D. Risk breakdown structure

10. As a project manager, you have invited experts for an effective brainstorming session to identify risks involved in the project. What is the ideal group size?
    A. 3   B. 6   C. 4   D. 5

11. Of the following personnel, who is NOT involved in project risk identification activities?
    A. Clerical staff
    B. Subject matter experts
    C. Other project managers
    D. Risk management experts

12. _____ is one of the tools/techniques used in risk identification.
    A. Risk tracker
    B. Checklist analysis
    C. Risk register
    D. Project scope

13. Jim is a project manager in a bank. He is collecting input for the risk identification process. What input would he be collecting to identify risks?
    I.   Project scope statement
    II. Enterprise environmental factors
    III. Project management plan
    IV. Diagramming techniques

    A. I and IV only
    B. III and IV only
    C. All of the above
    D. I, II and III only

14. Which of the following could a project manager collect from a risk tracker?
    I. Root causes of risk and updated risk categories
    II. List of identified risks
    III. Risk register
    IV. List of potential responses

    A. I and IV only
    B. III and IV only
    C. I, II and IV
    D. II only

14._____

15. The risk management plan should describe the entire risk management process, including auditing of the process, and should also define _____.
    A. reporting
    B. environmental factors
    C. organizational process assets
    D. project management plan

15._____

16. What do risk categories define?
    A. How to communicate risk activities and their results
    B. Types and sources of risks
    C. How risk management will be done on the process
    D. When and how the risk management activities appear in the project schedule

16._____

17. Which of the following is not a method of risk identification?
    A. Diagramming
    B. Interviewing
    C. SWOT
    D. RBS

17._____

18. Shauna is conducting a qualitative risk analysis for her project. What is she required to do?
    A. Apply a numerical rating to each risk
    B. Assess the probability and impact of each identified risk
    C. Assign each major risk to a risk owner
    D. Outline a course of action for each major risk identified

18._____

19. Which of the following is not a criterion to close a risk?
    A. Risk is no longer valid
    B. Risk event has occurred
    C. Risk activities are recorded regularly
    D. Risk closure at the direction of a project manager

19._____

20. As a project manager, you establish a risk contingency budget. Which of the following is not a purpose of establishing a risk contingency budget?
    A. To be reviewed as a standing agenda item for project team meetings
    B. To prepare in advance to manage the risks successfully
    C. To have some reserve funds
    D. To avoid going over the budget allotted

21. Which of the following statements is NOT correct in terms of designing a risk management?
    A. Risk is inherent to project work
    B. In any organization, projects will have common risks
    C. Some risks may occur more than once in the life a project
    D. Risks identified will definitely occur

22. All identified potential risk events that are viewed to be relevant to the project are to be recorded using the
    A. risk register
    B. risk management matrix
    C. risk report
    D. SOW

23. _____ is/are an example of a business risk.
    A. Poorly understood requirements
    B. A merger
    C. Introduction of new technology to the organization
    D. Work outside the project scope

24. Personnel turnover in a project is a
    A. Business risk
    B. Not a risk at all
    C. Technology risk
    D. Project risk

25. Which of the following is not an example of mitigation?
    A. Set expectations
    B. Involve customer in early planning process
    C. Provide training for personnel
    D. Hiring a backup person for a key team member

KEY (CORRECT ANSWERS)

1. D
2. B
3. D
4. C
5. C

6. B
7. B
8. A
9. A
10. A

11. A
12. B
13. D
14. C
15. A

16. B
17. D
18. B
19. C
20. A

21. D
22. B
23. B
24. D
25. D

TEST 3

DIRECTIONS: Each question or incomplete statement is followed by several suggested answers of completions. Select the one that best answers the question or complete the statement. *PRINT THE LETTER OF THE CORRECT ANSWER IN THE SPACE AT THE RIGHT.*

1. Project cost management deals with all the following EXCEPT:
    A. Estimating costs
    B. Budgeting
    C. Controlling costs
    D. Communicating costs

    1.____

2. Which of the following is not a process associated with project cost management?
    A. Control costs
    B. Maintain reserves
    C. Estimate costs
    D. Determine budget

    2.____

3. _____ is not a key deliverable of project cost processes.
    A. Cost performance baseline
    B. Activity cost estimates
    C. Results of estimates
    D. Work performance measurements

    3.____

4. As a project manager, you are calculating depreciation for an object. You are doing this by depreciating the same amount from the cost each year.
    What kind of depreciation technique are you applying?
    A. Sum of year depreciation
    B. Double-declining balance
    C. Multiple depreciation
    D. Straight line depreciation

    4.____

5. Which of the following is not a characteristic of analogous estimating?
    A. It is a top-down approach
    B. It is a form of an expert judgment
    C. It makes less time when compared to bottom-up estimation
    D. It is more accurate when compared to bottom-up estimation

    5.____

6. CPI = EV/AC. If CPI is less than 1, the project
    A. is over the budget
    B. is within the budget
    C. would be left over with unused budget
    D. efficiency is less

    6.____

7. Which of the following is not a tool used for estimating cost?
    A. Cost of quality
    B. Expert judgment
    C. Two point estimates
    D. Three point estimates

    7.____

8. What are the traditional project management triple constraints?
    A. Time, cost, resources
    B. Scope, cost, resources
    C. Scope, time, cost
    D. Resources, scope, budget

    8.____

9. Sam, an IT project manager, is having difficulty getting resources for his project, and hence has to depend highly on department heads. Which type of organization is Sam most likely working with?
    A. Functional
    B. Tight Matrix
    C. Weak Matrix
    D. Projectized

9.____

10. After-project costs are called _____.
    A. cost of quality
    B. extra costs
    C. life cycle costs
    D. over budget costs

10.____

11. Critical chain is a tool and technique for _____.
    A. developing schedule process
    B. defining critical path
    C. sequencing activities process
    D. estimating activity duration

11.____

12. The following are outputs for sequencing activities:
    A. Project schedule network diagram, Milestone list
    B. Project document updates, Project schedule network diagram
    C. Project schedule, Project document updates
    D. Schedule data, Schedule baseline

12.____

13. The schedule performance index is a measure of:
    A. Difference between earned value and planned value
    B. Ratio between earned value and planned value
    C. Difference between earned value and estimate at completion
    D. Ratio between estimate at completion and earned value

13.____

14. Which of the following is not an input, output or tools and technique for control schedule process?
    A. Project schedule, work performance measurements and variance analysis
    B. Project management plan, project document updates and schedule compression
    C. Work performance information, schedule baseline and schedule data
    D. Project schedule, change requests and resource leveling

14.____

15. Contracts, resource calendar, risk register and forecasts are all termed as
    A. inputs to administer procurements process
    B. outputs from close procurements process
    C. project documents
    D. tools and techniques of conduct procurement process

15.____

16. Fast tracking can be best described as
    A. one of the schedule compression techniques
    B. adding resources to activities on critical path
    C. shared or critical resources available only at specific times
    D. performing activities in parallel to shorten project duration

16.____

17. Which of the following contract types places the highest risk on the seller?
    A. Cost plus fixed fee
    B. Firm fixed price
    C. Cost plus incentive fee
    D. Time and material

18. Using the Power/Interest grid, a stakeholder with low power and having high interest on the project should be
    A. monitored
    B. managed closely
    C. kept satisfied
    D. kept informed

19. Stakeholder classification information is found in which of the following documents?
    A. Communications management plan
    B. Stakeholder register
    C. Stakeholder management strategy document
    D. Human resource plan

20. Thomas is a project manager of a well-reputed organization. One of your senior managers approaches you to explain constraints on labor utilization followed by a request to delay a couple of your projects. What is the best way to approach this situation?
    A. Agree with the senior manager and delay a couple of your projects
    B. Perform an impact analysis of the requested change
    C. Report the situation to the senior management and make a complaint against the senior manager
    D. Disagree with the senior manager and continue with the progress of the projects managed by you

21. Project management is defined as
    A. completion of a project
    B. gaining trust of the people involved in the project
    C. completing a WBS
    D. the application of specific knowledge, skills and tools

22. The most common form of dependency is
    A. Start to Start
    B. Finish to Start
    C. Finish to Finish
    D. Start to Finish

23. Kelly is a project manager who is in phase of project evaluation. Which of the following has to be considered during project evaluation phase?
    I. Give feedback to team members
    II. Learn from experiences
    III. Monitor
    IV. Celebrate

The correct answer(s) is/are:
  A. I only
  B. I, IV and III
  C. III only
  D. I, II and IV

24. Which of the following are very vital for the implementation of the project, and also must be repeated over and over during project's life.
    I.   Correct
    II. Monitor
    III. Estimate time and cost
    IV. Analyze

    The correct answer(s) is/are:
      A. I, II and III
      B. III only
      C. I, III and IV
      D. I, II and IV

25. What is the average amount of time is to be allocated to project planning?
      A. 10%
      B. 25%
      C. 22%
      D. 2%

KEY (CORRECT ANSWERS)

1. D
2. B
3. C
4. C
5. D

6. A
7. C
8. C
9. A
10. C

11. A
12. B
13. B
14. C
15. C

16. D
17. B
18. D
19. B
20. B

21. D
22. B
23. D
24. D
25. A

TEST 4

DIRECTIONS: Each question or incomplete statement is followed by several suggested answers of completions. Select the one that best answers the question or complete the statement. *PRINT THE LETTER OF THE CORRECT ANSWER IN THE SPACE AT THE RIGHT.*

1. Imagine you are assigned a project for which you do not have the required competency and experience to manage. What is the best plan of action?
    A. Make sure that you disclose any areas of improvement that need to be immediately addressed with the project sponsor before accepting the assignment
    B. Do not inform anyone about the gaps and learn as much as you can before any critical activity is due for delivery
    C. Consider the opportunity as a stepping stone for your career development and accept it
    D. Tell your boss that you cannot manage as you do not have the relevant experience and decline it

1.____

2. You are the project manager of a new project and are involved in selecting a vendor for acquiring products required for the project. Your close friend is running a company that is also very competitive and a reputed one along with other vendors who are competing for the bid. How can you handle this situation?
    A. Do not participate in the vendor selection process as this may be considered a conflict of interest
    B. Provide information to help your friend get the contract as you are the project manager of the project
    C. Do not inform anyone about your personal contact and be involved in the vendor selection process as normal
    D. Discuss with your project sponsor the possibility of a conflict of interest and leave the decision to him on the next steps

2.____

3. You have provided good guidance to your team members and this has resulted in successful execution of all of the phases involved. There was a particular phase that has been identified as very critical and the presence of a technical expert helped achieve this success. In the senior management review meeting you were credited with the success of the project, with specific mention of that particular phase. What do you do in this situation?
    A. Accept the appreciation and feel proud about the success of the project
    B. Do not mention anything about the technical expert role as you were the project manager for this project
    C. Give credit to the technical expert and let the senior management know how the presence of the technical expert helped the team to be successful
    D. Accept the appreciation from the senior management and thank the technical expert in private for achieving this success

3.____

4. As a project manager you are preparing status reports for a meeting with the stakeholders. One of your team members has come out with an issue that will cause some delay in the project timeline. You have a plan that can be implemented to make sure that this issue can be managed without causing any delay in the timeline, but you currently do not have the time to update the project plan. How will you handle this situation?
    A. Present the status of the project as *on-track* without discussing anything about this issue as you will have time to prepare before the next meeting
    B. Cancel the meeting as you do not have the time to update the details to be provided to the stakeholders
    C. Present the status of the project *as-is* without minimizing the effect of the delay and discuss details of the planned approach to solve this issue
    D. Fire your team that is responsible for causing this delay as it has created a bad impression of you amongst the stakeholders

5. John is an Associate Director in a pharmaceutical company managing its internal projects. He has presented whitepapers on project execution methodologies and is highly respected within the organization. He also regularly conducts workshops & lectures in coordination with PMO. What kind of power does John possess?
    A. Referent power
    B. Coercive power
    C. Reward power
    D. Expert power

6. You are a project manager working for a non-profit organization. You had been assigned a project that is in the initial stage and involves development of an eco-system in a large community. You are reviewing the deliverables and templates from similar projects that are available in the company lessons learnt knowledge base. Which item will be of much importance to you?
    A. Project Information Management System
    B. Enterprise Environmental Factors
    C. Organization Process Assets
    D. Standard Templates

7. A project that you were managing is nearing completion. As part of the deliverables you are required to complete lessons-learned documentation of the project. What is the primary purpose of creating lessons-learned documentation?
    A. Provide information of project success
    B. Help identify all the failures
    C. Provide information on minimizing negative impacts and maximizing positive events for future projects of similar nature
    D. Comply with the organization's objectives

8. You are managing project teams that work from different locations and there has been issues with the teams' ability to effectively perform. This has resulted in delay in timeline. Which kind of team development technique would be most effective in this situation?
    A. Mediation
    B. Training
    C. Co-location
    D. Rewards

9. The project sponsor has requested that you create a project charter for a new project that you will manage next month. Which document will you utilize to create the project charter that will justify the need for the project?
    A. Project SOW
    B. Business Need
    C. Business Case
    D. Cost-benefit Analysis

10. An audit is being performed by a team for the project you are managing. The team reports that the standards utilized need to be analyzed as several processes that are not relevant to the current project.
What is the process that the team is currently involved?
    A. Quality planning
    B. Quality control
    C. Quality assurance
    D. Benchmark creation

11. The change control board of your organization has approved changes that were submitted and the project team is executing them.
What would this process be considered?
    A. Executing the change request
    B. Implementing a corrective action
    C. Gold-plating
    D. Approving the change request

12. Which is the primary technique that is carried out to ensure that a contract award is executed correctly or not?
    A. Litigation
    B. Contract negotiation
    C. Inspections
    D. Procurement audit

13. In the final stages of completing a project, you and your team are involved in creating the project report that will be presented to the stakeholders. Which of the following information is not appropriate to be included in the final report?
    A. Recommendations from your team
    B. Project success factors
    C. WBS dictionary
    D. Details of the process improvements

14. At the completion of a project, your team has completed the lessons-learned documentation and archived in the database. Who should have access to these documents?
    A. Project team members
    B. Operations department
    C. All of the company's members
    D. Functional managers

15. You are project manager for a large project that is in the final stages of completion and you need to formally provide information on the major milestone achieved. You are also in need of immediate feedback from the stakeholders. Which is the best communication method to meet this requirement?
    A. E-mail
    B. Web publishing
    C. Meeting
    D. Videoconferencing

16. Which document will formally authorize a project manager to start the project?
    A. Project SOW
    B. Project Charter
    C. Business Case
    D. Stakeholder Register

17. Which of the following documents would be utilized to ascertain the project's investment worthiness?
    A. Project Charter
    B. Business Case
    C. Business Need
    D. Procurement documents

18. Which of the following conflict resolution is considered as Lose-lose solution?
    A. Problem-solving
    B. Forcing
    C. Compromising
    D. Withdrawing

19. McGregor's Theory states that all workers fit into one of the two groups. Which of the following theories believes that people are willing to work on their own and need less supervision?
    A. Theory X
    B. Theory Y
    C. Maslow's Hierarchy
    D. Expectancy

20. The major cause for conflicts on a project are schedule, project priorities and _____.
    A. cost
    B. resources
    C. personality
    D. management

21. The project manager is responsible for
    A. the success of the project
    B. achieving the project objectives
    C. authorizing the project
    D. performing the project work

22. Which of the following actions correspond to reducing the consequences of future problems?
    A. Corrective action
    B. Preventive action
    C. Defect repair
    D. Change request

23. As a project manager for a large-scale project, you are in the process of procuring materials required for the project. Which of the following documents will you not be responsible for?
    A. Procurement documents
    B. Procurement statements of work
    C. Source selection criteria
    D. Proposals

24. During which process group will the detailed requirements be gathered?
    A. Initiating
    B. Planning
    C. Executing
    D. Closing

25. The values that illustrate PMIs code of ethics and professional conduct are
    A. respect, honesty, responsibility and honorability
    B. honesty, cultural diversity, integrity and responsibility
    C. fairness, responsibility, honesty and respect
    D. honorability, fairness, respect and responsibility

KEY (CORRECT ANSWERS)

1. A
2. D
3. C
4. C
5. D

6. C
7. C
8. C
9. C
10. C

11. A
12. D
13. C
14. C
15. D

16. B
17. B
18. C
19. B
20. B

21. B
22. B
23. D
24. B
25. C

EXAMINATION SECTION
TEST 1

DIRECTIONS: Each question or incomplete statement is followed by several suggested answers of completions. Select the one that BEST answers the question or Complete the statement. *PRINT THE LETTER OF THE CORRECT ANSWER IN THE SPACE AT THE RIGHT.*

1. An accepted deadline for a project approaches. However, the project manager realizes only 85% of the work has been completed. The project manager then issues a change request.
   What should the change request authorize?

   A. Corrective action based on causes
   B. Escalation approval to use contingency funding
   C. Additional resources using the contingency fund
   D. Team overtime to meet schedule

   1._____

2. _____ is a valid tool or technique to assist the project manager to assure the success of the process improvement plan.

   A. Benchmarking
   B. Change control system
   C. Process analysis
   D. Configuration management system

   2._____

3. A project manager meets with the project team to review lessons learned from previous projects. In what activity is the team involved?

   A. Performance management
   B. Project team status meeting
   C. Scope identification
   D. Risk identification

   3._____

4. _____ process helps you to purchase goods from external suppliers.

   A. Quality management
   B. Procurement management
   C. Cost management
   D. Communication management

   4._____

5. Which of the following is not involved in procurement management?

   A. Review supplier performance against contract
   B. Identify and resolve supplier performance issues
   C. Communicate the status to management
   D. Manage a WBS

   5._____

6. _____ contract is advantageous to a buyer.

   A. Fixed price
   B. Cost reimbursable
   C. Time and material
   D. Fixed price plus incentive

   6._____

7. Which of the following contracts is advantageous to a seller?   7.____

    A. Fixed price
    B. Cost reimbursable
    C. Time and material
    D. Fixed price plus incentive

8. Tom is a manager of a project whose deliverable has many uncertainties associated with it. What kind of contract should he use during the procurement process?   8.____

    A. Fixed price
    B. Cost reimbursable
    C. Time and material
    D. Fixed price plus incentive

9. Cost plus _____ is not a cost-reimbursable contract.   9.____

    A. fixed fee
    B. fee
    C. fixed time
    D. incentive fee

10. _____ type of contract helps both the seller and buyer to save, if the performance criteria are exceeded.   10.____

    A. Cost plus fixed fee
    B. Cost plus fee
    C. Cost plus fixed time
    D. Cost plus incentive fee

11. A project manager with a construction company. She has to complete a project in a specified time, but does have enough time to send the job out for bids. What type of contract would save her time?   11.____

    A. Fixed price
    B. Cost reimbursable
    C. Time and material
    D. Fixed price plus incentive

12. The major type(s) of standard warranty (ies) that are used in the business environment is (are):   12.____

    A. express
    B. negotiated
    C. implied
    D. A and C

13. During contract management, the project manager must consider the   13.____

    A. acquisition process and contract administration
    B. contract administration and ecological environment
    C. ecological environment and acquisition process
    D. offer, acceptance and consideration

14. Which contract type places the most risk on the seller?   14._____

    A. Cost plus percentage fee
    B. Cost plus incentive fee
    C. Cost plus fixed fee
    D. Firm fixed price

15. Finalizing project close-out happens when a project manager   15._____

    A. archives the project records
    B. completes the contract
    C. complete lessons learned
    D. reassigns the team

16. Unit price contract is fair to both owner and contractor,   16._____

    A. as the actual volumes will be measured and paid as the work proceeds
    B. as the owner will provide bill of quantities
    C. as both are absorbing an equal amount of risk
    D. all of the above

17. Bill is the manager of a project that requires different areas of expertise.   17._____
    Which one of the following contracts should he sign?

    A. Fixed price
    B. Cost reimbursable
    C. Time and material
    D. Unit price

18. Which of the following contracts is commonly used in projects that involve pilot   18._____
    programs or harness new technologies?

    A. Fixed price
    B. Incentive
    C. Time and material
    D. Unit price

19. Procurement cycle involves all of the following steps EXCEPT   19._____

    A. supplier contract
    B. renewal
    C. sending a proposal
    D. information gathering

20. What would happen if a project manager does not take up a background review during the   20._____
    procurement process?

    A. Price might not be negotiated
    B. Credibility of the goods might not be validated
    C. Goods might not be shipped
    D. Both A and B

21. _____ is not a part of a procurement document.

    A. Buyer's commencement to the bid
    B. Summons by the financially responsible party
    C. Establishing terms and conditions of a contract
    D. Roles of responsibilities of internal team

22. Which of the following is NOT an example of a procurement document?

    A. Offers
    B. Contracts
    C. Project record archives
    D. Request for quotation

23. A project manager needs to follow _____ for a good procurement document to be drafted.

    A. clear definition of the responsibilities, rights and commitments of both parties in the contract
    B. clear definition of the nature and quality of the goods or services to be provided
    C. clear and easy to understand language
    D. all of the above

24. Which of the following is not a concern with respect to procurement management?

    A. Reassigning the team
    B. Not all goods and services that a business requires need to be purchased from outside
    C. You would need to have a good idea of what you exactly require and then go on to consider various options and alternatives
    D. You would need to consider different criteria, apart from just the cost, to finally decide on which supplier you would want to go with.

25. Source qualifications are a part of the _____ phase of Acquisition Process Cycle.

    A. post-award
    B. pre-award
    C. award
    D. origination

KEY (CORRECT ANSWERS)

1. A
2. C
3. D
4. B
5. D

6. A
7. B
8. B
9. C
10. D

11. C
12. D
13. A
14. D
15. B

16. C
17. D
18. B
19. C
20. B

21. D
22. C
23. D
24. A
25. C

TEST 2

DIRECTIONS: Each question or incomplete statement is followed by several suggested answers of completions. Select the one that BEST answers the question or Complete the statement. *PRINT THE LETTER OF THE CORRECT ANSWER IN THE SPACE AT THE RIGHT.*

1. Which of the following project tools details the project scope?

    A. Project plan
    B. Gantt chart
    C. Milestone checklist
    D. Score cards

    1._____

2. Which of the following is NOT a project tool?

    A. Gantt chart
    B. Milestone checklist
    C. Score cards
    D. MS project

    2._____

3. _____ is accompanied by project audits by a third party. As a result, non-compliance and action items are tracked.

    A. Gantt chart
    B. Milestone checklist
    C. Project reviews
    D. Delivery reviews

    3._____

4. An IT project manager, is involved in tracking his team's performance. Which tool would he use to gauge this performance?

    A. Score cards
    B. Gantt chart
    C. Project management software
    D. Milestone checklist

    4._____

5. What tool does a manager use to track the interdependencies of each project activity?

    A. Project plan
    B. Gantt chart
    C. Project management software
    D. Milestone checklist

    5._____

6. Which tool would be used for a manager to determine if he or she is on track in terms of project progress?

    A. Project management software
    B. Delivery reviews
    C. Project reviews
    D. Milestone checklist

    6._____

7. Which of the following tools is used for individual member promotion? 7._____

    A. Delivery reviews
    B. Score cards
    C. Project reviews
    D. Milestone checklist

8. Which of the following is NOT a project management process? 8._____

    A. Project planning
    B. Project initiation
    C. Project management software
    D. Closeout and evaluation

9. _____ is the phase in which the service provider proves the eligibility and ability of completing the project to the client. 9._____

    A. Pre-sale period
    B. Project execution
    C. Sign-off
    D. Closeout and evaluation

10. Controlling of the project could be done by following all of the following protocols EXCEPT 10._____

    A. communication plan
    B. quality assurance test plan
    C. test plan
    D. project plan

11. A manager wants his project to be successful and hence verifies the successful outcome of every activity leading to successful completion of the project. Which of the following activities would he use to do so? 11._____

    A. Control
    B. Test plan
    C. Project plan
    D. Validation

12. What happens during the closeout and evaluation phase? 12._____

    A. Evaluation of the entire project
    B. Hand over the implemented system
    C. Identifying mistakes and taking necessary action
    D. All of the above

13. A project manager, is conducting validation and verification functions. Which team's assistance would she need in order to do so? 13._____

    A. Quality assurance team
    B. Project team
    C. Client team
    D. Third-party vendor

14. Tracking the effort and cost of the project is done during _____.

    A. project execution
    B. control and validation
    C. closeout and evaluation
    D. communication plan

15. _____ is the entity created for governing the processes, practices, tools and other activities related to project management in an organization.

    A. Project management office
    B. Project management software
    C. Quality assurance
    D. None of the above

16. A project management office must be built with the following considerations EXCEPT

    A. process optimization
    B. productivity enhancement
    C. building the bottom line of their organization
    D. none of the above

17. An advantage of a project management office is that it

    A. helps cut down staff
    B. helps cut down resources
    C. refines the processes related to project management
    D. all of the above

18. A project management office could fail because of

    A. lack of executive management support
    B. incapability
    C. it adds figures to the bottom line of the company
    D. both A and B

19. _____ is used to analyze the difficulties that may arise due to the execution of the project.

    A. Project management office
    B. Project management triangle
    C. Both A and B
    D. None of the above

20. The three constraints in a project management triangle are _____.

    A. time, cost and scope
    B. time, resources and quality
    C. time, resources and people
    D. time, resources and cost

21. A project manager, is experiencing challenges related to project triangle and hence finds difficulty in achieving the project objectives. Which of the following skills would help her?

    A. Time management
    B. Effective communication
    C. Managing people
    D. All of the above

22. _____ is NOT a role of a project manager.

    A. Carrying out basic project tasks
    B. Keeping stakeholders informed on the project progress
    C. Defining project scope and assigning tasks to team members
    D. Setting objectives

23. Kathy is advising Nicole on the goals and challenges a project manager must consider. Which of the following should she discuss?

    A. Deadlines
    B. Client satisfaction
    C. No budget overrun
    D. All of the above

24. Team management deals with all of the following EXCEPT

    A. providing incentives and encouragement
    B. maintaining warm and friendly relationship with teammates
    C. meeting requirements of the client
    D. including them in project related decisions

25. _____ is vital to win client satisfaction.

    A. Finishing the work on scheduled time
    B. Ensuring that most standards are met
    C. Having a limited relationship with the client
    D. All of the above

KEY (CORRECT ANSWERS)

1. A
2. D
3. C
4. A
5. B

6. D
7. B
8. C
9. A
10. C

11. D
12. D
13. A
14. A
15. A

16. D
17. C
18. D
19. B
20. A

21. D
22. A
23. D
24. C
25. A

TEST 3

DIRECTIONS: Each question or incomplete statement is followed by several suggested answers of completions. Select the one that BEST answers the question or Complete the statement. *PRINT THE LETTER OF THE CORRECT ANSWER IN THE SPACE AT THE RIGHT.*

1. What type of strategy is followed by a manager before his workforce focuses on with performance?

    A. Activators
    B. Behaviors
    C. Consequences
    D. Deviators

    1._____

2. _____ define how the workforce performs or behaves within the activity or situation as a result of activators or consequences.

    A. Deviators
    B. Consequences
    C. Behaviors
    D. Activators

    2._____

3. _____ explain how the manager handles the workforce after the performance.

    A. Deviators
    B. Consequences
    C. Behaviors
    D. Activators

    3._____

4. Which of the following is found to have a great impact on workforce behavior?

    A. Deviators
    B. Consequences
    C. Behaviors
    D. Activators

    4._____

5. Nancy, an IT project manager, is keen to delegate her work. She is aware that a good manager's role is about delegating work effectively in order to complete the task. What should she consider before delegating?

    A. Delegating the work with clear instructions and expectations stated
    B. Providing enough moral support
    C. Identify individuals that are capable of carrying out a particular task
    D. All the above

    5._____

6. Which of the following is NOT a tool related to controlling and assuring quality?

    A. Check sheet
    B. Cause-and-effect diagram
    C. Activators
    D. Scatter diagram

    6._____

7. _____ are used for understanding business, implementation and organizational problems.

    A. Cause-and-effect diagrams
    B. Scatter diagrams
    C. Control charts
    D. Pareto charts

    7._____

8. Jim is replacing the earlier project manager in the middle of the project and hard-pressed with time. He has to work on a priority basis.
   Which of the following tools would he use to identify priorities?

   A. Cause-and-effect diagram
   B. Scatter diagram
   C. Control chart
   D. Pareto chart

Questions 9-11 refer to the following chart.

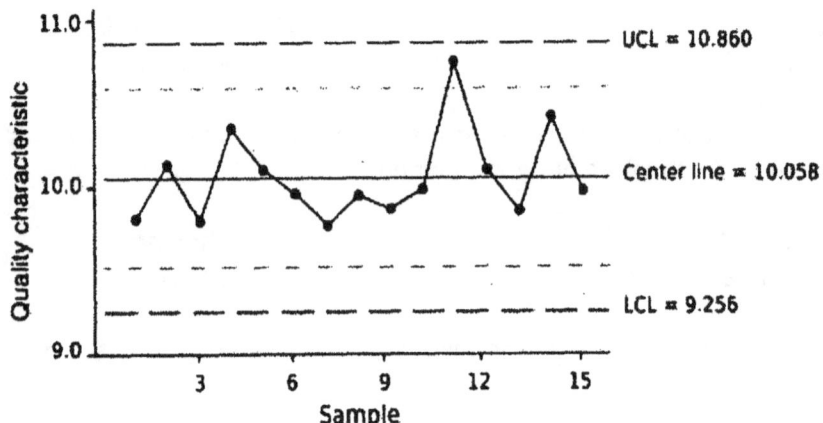

9. What type of tool is this?

   A. Control chart
   B. Flow chart
   C. Scatter diagram
   D. Pareto chart

10. The above-mentioned chart/tool is used for _____.

    A. identifying sets of priorities
    B. comparing two variables
    C. monitoring the performance of a process
    D. gathering and organizing data

11. The above chart/tool could be used to identify all of the following EXCEPT

    A. the stability of the process
    B. the common cause of variation
    C. the parameter(s) that have the highest impact on the specific concern
    D. conditions where the monitoring team needs to react

12. Which of the following tools would a project manager use to perform a trend analysis?

    A. Flow chart
    B. Scatter diagram
    C. Cause-and-effect diagram
    D. Pareto chart

13. _____ is/are a common and simple method used by project managers to arrive at an effective cause-and-effect diagram.

    A. Survey
    B. Brainstorming
    C. Informal discussions
    D. Formal presentations

14. Which of the following tools should a project manager use to gain a brief understanding of the project's critical path?

    A. Flow chart
    B. Pareto chart
    C. Histogram
    D. Check sheet

15. _____ is NOT a step involved in the benchmarking process.

    A. Planning
    B. Analysis of data
    C. Monitoring
    D. None of the above

16. As a project manager, where will you collect primary data when you collect information?

    i) Benchmarked company
    ii) Press
    iii) Publication
    iv) Website

    A. Only I
    B. Both I and II
    C. I, II, III and IV
    D. Both I and IV

17. Which of the following methods is recommended to conduct primary research?

    A. E-mail
    B. Referring to the website of other companies
    C. Telephone
    D. Face-to-face interviews

18. Analysis of data involves all of the following EXCEPT

    A. sharing data with all the stakeholders
    B. data presentation
    C. results projection
    D. classifying the performance gaps in processes

19. _____ is referred to as an enabler, which will help project managers to act wisely.

   A. Projection of results
   B. Performance gap identification
   C. Root cause of performance gaps
   D. Presentation of data

20. Which of the following needs to be done in order to monitor the quality of the project?

   A. Evaluating the progress made
   B. Reiterating the impact of change
   C. Making necessary adjustments
   D. All the above

Use the following cause-and-effect diagram to answer questions 21 through 23.

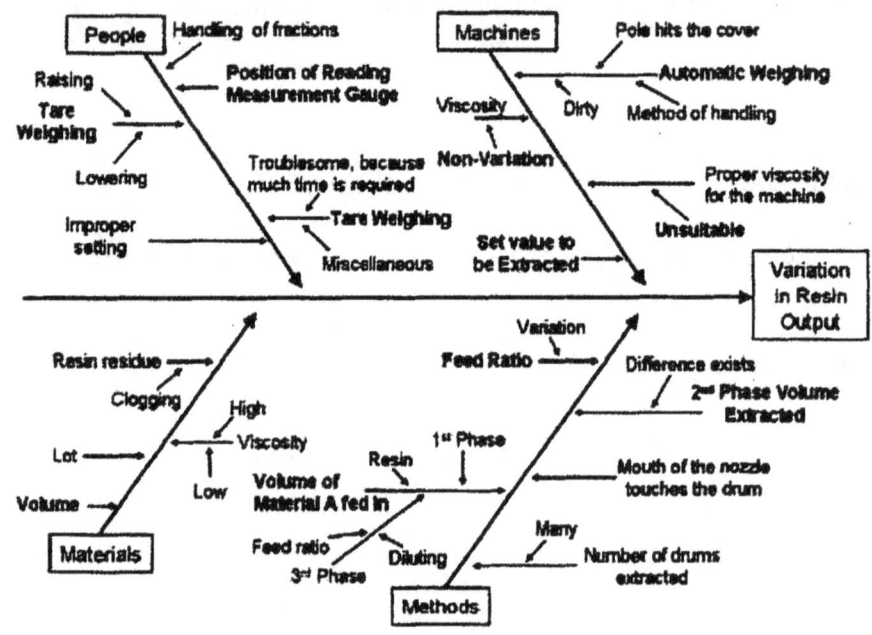

21. Which of the following is NOT represented in this diagram?

   A. Problem
   B. Major cause of the problem
   C. Contributing factors
   D. Possible causes of the problem

22. What is the effect with respect to the diagram?

   A. Materials
   B. Methods
   C. Variation in Resin Output
   D. People

23. As a project manager, what will you do to gain a better understanding of the problems and handling them?

    A. Investigations
    B. Surveys
    C. Interviews
    D. All the above

24. Kotter's change management process involves all the following steps EXCEPT

    A. building a team
    B. resource management
    C. creating a vision
    D. removing obstacles

25. _____ lets team members know why they are working on a change initiative.

    A. Removing obstacles
    B. Building a team
    C. Integrating the change
    D. Creating a vision

KEY (CORRECT ANSWERS)

1. A	11. C
2. C	12. B
3. B	13. B
4. B	14. A
5. D	15. D
6. C	16. C
7. A	17. B
8. D	18. A
9. A	19. C
10. C	20. D

21. B
22. C
23. D
24. B
25. D

TEST 4

DIRECTIONS: Each question or incomplete statement is followed by several suggested answers of completions. Select the one that best answers the question or Complete the statement. *PRINT THE LETTER OF THE CORRECT ANSWER IN THE SPACE AT THE RIGHT.*

1. Which of the following is NOT a communication blocker?
    A. Judging
    B. Accusing
    C. Globalizing
    D. Listening

    1._____

2. Using words like "always" and "never" is an example of _____.
    A. judging
    B. accusing
    C. globalizing
    D. listening

    2._____

3. What should you do as a project manager to eliminate communication blockers?
    A. Encourage others to avoid communication blockers by educating them
    B. Be aware of the various blockers and take steps to remove them
    C. Model to promote effective and empathetic communication
    D. All of the above

    3._____

4. What would happen if there were no proper communication channel?
    A. Inefficient flow of information
    B. Clarity among employees on what is expected of them
    C. Sense of company mind/common vision among employees
    D. Clarity among employees on the happening within the company

    4._____

5. As a project manager, you could use any one of the following types of language EXCEPT _____ for communicating with your team.
    A. formal
    B. insulting
    C. informal
    D. unofficial

    5._____

6. A(n) _____ is/are NOT an example of formal communication.
    A. annual report
    B. business plan
    C. social gathering
    D. review meetings

    6._____

7. _____ types of communication are used to communicate company policies, goals and procedures.
    A. Formal
    B. Informal
    C. Unofficial
    D. None of the above

8. _____ is NOT an example of informal communication.
    A. Survey
    B. Quality circle
    C. Team work
    D. Training program

9. "Grapevine" is an example of _____ communication.
    A. Formal
    B. Informal
    C. Unofficial
    D. None of the above

10. What question would you NOT consider as a project manager before choosing the right method to communicate?
    A. Who is the target audience?
    B. Will it lead to employee productivity?
    C. What kind of information would be helpful for clarity among employees?
    D. Which is the best way to threaten the employees?

11. Which of the following is not included in "The Five Ws of Communication Management"?
    A. What information would prompt employees to work out of fear?
    B. What information is essential for the project?
    C. What is the time required for the communication to happen effectively?
    D. Who requires information and what type of information is required?

12. _____ refers to developing a message.
    A. Decoding
    B. Encoding
    C. Transmission
    D. Feedback

13. _____ refers to interpreting the message.
    A. Decoding
    B. Encoding
    C. Transmission
    D. Feedback

14. Which of the following is not necessarily involved in a communication process?
    A. Sender
    B. Transmission
    C. Vision
    D. Receiver

15. _____ is NOT a sign of active listening.
    A. Making eye contact
    B. Asking questions to gain clarity
    C. Using gestures like nodding head
    D. Using gestures that distract the speaker

16. Madeline is a project manager and involved in conflict management. Which of the following should she use to manage a conflict?
    A. Identify actions that resolve conflicts
    B. Identify actions that would aggravate conflicts
    C. Consider different methods of resolving the conflict
    D. All the above

17. A managerial action that would NOT aggravate conflict is _____.
    A. poor communication
    B. assertive style of leadership
    C. ill-defined expectations
    D. authoritative style of leadership

18. An example of a managerial action that would NOT minimize a conflict is
    A. well-defined job descriptions
    B. participative approach
    C. submissive style of leadership
    D. fostering team spirit

19. Which of the following methods could you use as a project manager to handle conflicts?   19.____
    A. Flight
    B. Fake
    C. Fight
    D. All of the above

20. _____ is the term used when people run away from problems instead of confronting them and turn to avoidance as a means of handling conflict.   20.____
    A. Flight
    B. Fake
    C. Fight
    D. Fold

21. _____ is the term used when an individual is made to agree to a solution by means of browbeating.   21.____
    A. Flight
    B. Fake
    C. Fight
    D. Fold

22. Which of the following is NOT a step in conflict management?   22.____
    A. Choose the best solution that satisfy most people most of the time and implement this
    B. Engage in participatory dialogue and find a range of solutions that will be acceptable to all the parties concerned
    C. Eliminate those who promote mutual understanding and acceptance
    D. Identify the limiting resource or constraint that is generally at the root cause of the conflict

23. Which of the following is NOT a skill required for conflict resolution?   23.____
    A. Clarity in communication
    B. Aggressiveness
    C. Negotiation
    D. Listening

24. _____ is essential to be prepared for any problems that may arise when it is least expected.   24.____
    A. Conflict management
    B. Communication management
    C. Crisis management
    D. None of the above

25. Which of the following is NOT a type of crisis?
    A. Financial
    B. Technological
    C. Natural
    D. Negotiation

25._____

KEY (CORRECT ANSWERS)

1. D
2. C
3. D
4. A
5. B

6. C
7. A
8. A
9. C
10. D

11. A
12. B
13. A
14. C
15. D

16. D
17. B
18. C
19. D
20. A

21. D
22. C
23. B
24. C
25. D

EXAMINATION SECTION
TEST 1

DIRECTIONS: Each question or incomplete statement is followed by several suggested answers or completions. Select the one that BEST answers the question or completes the statement. *PRINT THE LETTER OF THE CORRECT ANSWER IN THE SPACE AT THE RIGHT.*

1. Which one of the following is LEAST likely to be an area or cause of trouble in the use of staff personnel?

    A. Misunderstanding of the role the staff personnel are supposed to play as a result of vagueness of definition of their duties and authority
    B. Tendency of staff personnel almost always to be older than line personnel at comparable salary levels with whom they must deal
    C. Selection of staff personnel who fail to have simultaneously both competence in their specialities and skill in staff work
    D. The staff person fails to understand mixed staff and operating duties

    1._____

2. Which of the following is generally NOT a valid statement with respect to the supervisory process?

    A. General supervision is more effective than close supervision.
    B. Employee-centered supervisors lead more effectively than do production-centered supervisors.
    C. Employee satisfaction is directly related to productivity.
    D. Low-producing supervisors use techniques that are different from high-producing supervisors.

    2._____

3. Which of the following is the MOST essential element for proper evaluation of the performance of subordinate supervisors?

    A. Careful definition of each supervisor's specific job responsibilities and of his progress in meeting mutually agreed upon work goals
    B. System of rewards and penalties based on each supervisor's progress in meeting clearly defined performance standards
    C. Definition of personality traits, such as industry, initiative, dependability, and cooperativeness, required for effective job performance
    D. Breakdown of each supervisor's job into separate components and a rating of his performance on each individual task

    3._____

4. The PRINCIPAL advantage of specialization for the operating efficiency of a public service agency is that specialization

    A. reduces the amount of red tape in coordinating the activities of mutually dependent departments
    B. simplifies the problem of developing adequate job controls
    C. provides employees with a clear understanding of the relationship of their activities to the overall objectives of the agency
    D. reduces destructive competition for power between departments

    4._____

5. A list of conditions which encourages good morale inside a work group would NOT include a

   A. high rate of agreement among group members on values and objectives
   B. tight control system to minimize the risk of individual error
   C. good possibility that joint action will accomplish goals
   D. past history of successful group accomplishment

6. Of the following, the MOST important factor to be considered in selecting a training strategy or program is the

   A. requirements of the job to be performed by the trainees
   B. educational level or prior training of the trainees
   C. size of the training group
   D. quality and competence of available training specialists

7. Of the following, the one which is considered to be LEAST characteristic of the higher ranks of management is

   A. that higher levels of management benefit from modern technology
   B. that success is measured by the extent to which objectives are achieved
   C. the number of subordinates that directly report to a manager
   D. the de-emphasis of individual and specialized performance

8. Assume that a manager is preparing a training syllabus to be used in training members of her staff.
   Which of the following would NOT be a valid principle of the learning process to consider when preparing this training syllabus?

   A. When a person has thoroughly learned a task, it takes a lot of effort to create a little more improvement.
   B. In complicated learning situations, there is a period in which an additional period of practice produces an equal amount of improvement in learning.
   C. The less a person knows about the task, the slower the initial progress.
   D. The more a person knows about the task, the slower the initial progress.

9. Which statement BEST illustrates when collective bargaining agreements are working well?

   A. Executives strongly support subordinate managers.
   B. The management rights clause in the contract is clear and enforced.
   C. Contract provisions are competently interpreted.
   D. The provisions of the agreement are properly interpreted, communicated, and observed.

10. An executive who wishes to encourage subordinates to communicate freely with him about a job-related problem should FIRST

   A. state his own position on the problem before listening to the subordinates' ideas
   B. invite subordinates to give their own opinions on the problem
   C. ask subordinates for their reactions to his own ideas about the problem
   D. guard the confidentiality of management information about the problem

11. The ability to deal constructively with intra-organizational conflict is an essential attribute of the successful manager.
The one of the following types of conflict which would be LEAST difficult to handle constructively is a situation in which there is

   A. agreement on objectives, but disagreement as to the probable results of adopting the various alternatives
   B. agreement on objectives, disagreement on alternative courses of action, and relative certainty as to the outcome of one of the alternatives
   C. disagreement on objectives and on alternative courses of action, and relative certainty as to the outcome of one of the alternatives
   D. disagreement on objectives and on alternative courses of action, but uncertainty as to the outcome of the alternatives

12. Which of the following actions does NOT belong in a properly conducted grievance handling process?

   A. Gathering relevant information on why the grievance arose
   B. Formulating a personal judgment about the fairness or unfairness of the grievance at the time the grievance is presented
   C. Establishing tentative answers to the grievance
   D. Following up to see whether the solution has eliminated the difficulty

13. Grievances are generally defined as complaints expressed over work-related matters.
Which one of the following is MOST important for managers to be aware of in connection with this definition?
The

   A. fact that the definition fails to separate the subject of the grievance from the attitude of the grievant
   B. fact that anything in the organization may be the source of the grievance
   C. need to assume that dissatisfied people have adverse effects on productivity
   D. implication that management should be concerned about expressed grievances and unconcerned about unexpressed grievances

14. In carrying out disciplinary action, the MOST important procedure for all managers to follow is to

   A. convince all levels of management on the need for discipline from the organization's viewpoint
   B. follow up on a disciplinary action and not assume that the action has been effective
   C. convince all executives that proper discipline is a legitimate tool for their use
   D. convince all executives that they need to display confidence in the organization's rules

15. Assume that an employee under your supervision is acquitted in court of criminal charges arising out of his employment.
    Of the following statements concerning disciplinary action, which is MOST NEARLY correct?

   A. Disciplinary proceedings against the employee may not be held for the same offenses on which he was tried and acquitted.
   B. In a disciplinary action, the acquittal dispenses with the requirement that the employee be advised as to his constitutional rights.
   C. Civil Rights Law Section 79 prohibits the taking of any further punitive action by an employer if the offense did not involve official corruption.
   D. It is possible for the employee to be found guilty of the same offense when tried in a departmental hearing.

16. Work rules can be an effective tool in the process of personnel management.
    The BEST practical definition for work rules is that they are

   A. minimum standards of conduct or performance that apply to individuals or groups at work in an organization
   B. prescriptions that serve to specialize employee behavior
   C. predetermined decisions about disciplinary action
   D. the major determinant of an organization's climate and the morale of its workforce

Questions 17-18

DIRECTIONS: Questions 17 and 18 pertain to identification of words that are incorrectly used because they are not in keeping with the meaning of the quotation. In answering each question, the first step is to read the passage and identify the incorrectly used word, and then select the word which, when substituted, BEST serves to convey the meaning of the quotation.

17. Among the Housing Manager's overall responsibilities in administering a project is the prevention of the development of conditions which might lead to termination of tenancy and eviction of a tenant. Where there appears to be doubt that a tenant is fully aware of his responsibilities and is thus jeopardizing his tenancy, the Housing Manager should acquaint him with these responsibilities. Where a situation involves behavior of a tenant or a member of his family, the Housing Manager should confirm, through discussions and referrals to social agencies, correction of the conditions before they reach a state where there is no alternative but termination proceedings.

    A. Coordinate
    B. Identify
    C. Assert
    D. Attempt

17._____

18. The one universal administrative complaint is that the budget is inadequate. Between adequacy and inadequacy lie all degrees of adequacy. Further, human wants are modest in relation to human resources. From these two facts we may conclude that the fundamental criterion of administrative decision must be a criterion of efficiency (the degree to which the goals have been reached relative to the available resources) rather than a criterion of adequacy (the degree to which its goals have been reached). The task of the manager is to maximize social values relative to limited resources.

    A. Improve
    B. Simple
    C. Limitless
    D. Optimize

18._____

Questions 19-21.

DIRECTIONS: Questions 19 through 21 are to be answered SOLELY on the basis of the following situation.

John Foley, a top administrator, is responsible for output in his organization. Because productivity had been lagging for two periods in a row, Foley decided to establish a committee of his subordinate managers to investigate the reasons for the poor performance and to make recommendations for improvements. After two meetings, the committee came to the conclusions and made the recommendations that follow.

Output forecasts had been handed down from the top without prior consultation with middle management and first level supervision. Lines of authority and responsibility had been unclear. The planning and control process should be decentralized.

After receiving the committee's recommendations, Foley proceeded to take the following actions. Foley decided he would retain final authority to establish quotas but would delegate to the middle managers the responsibility for meeting quotas.

After receiving Foley's decision, the middle managers proceeded to delegate to the first-line supervisors the authority to establish their own quotas. The middle managers eventually received and combined the first-line supervisors' quotas so that these conformed to Foley's.

19. Foley's decision to delegate responsibility for meeting quotas to the middle managers is inconsistent with sound management principles because

    A. Foley should not have involved himself in the first place
    B. middle managers do not have the necessary skills
    C. quotas should be established by the chief executive
    D. responsibility should not be delegated

20. The principle of co-extensiveness of responsibility and authority bears on Foley's decision.
    In this case, it implies that

    A. authority should exceed responsibility
    B. authority should be delegated to match the degree of responsibility
    C. both authority and responsibility should be retained and not delegated
    D. responsibility should be delegated, but authority should be retained

21. The middle managers' decision to delegate to the first-line supervisors the authority to establish quotas was INCORRECTLY reasoned because

    A. delegation and control must go together
    B. first-line supervisors are in no position to establish quotas
    C. one cannot delegate authority that one does not possess
    D. the meeting of quotas should not be delegated

22. If one attempts to list the advantages of the management-by-exception principle as it is used in connection with the budgeting process, several distinct advantages could be cited.
    Which of the following is NOT an advantage of this principle as it applies to the budgeting process?
    Management-by-exception

    A. saves time
    B. identifies critical problem areas
    C. focuses attention and concentrates effort
    D. escalates the frequency and importance of budget-related decisions

23. The MOST accurate description of a budget is that

    A. a budget is made up by an organization to plan its future activities
    B. a budget specifies in dollars and cents how much is spent in a particular time period
    C. a budget specifies how much the organization to which it relates estimates it will spend over a certain period of time
    D. all plans dealing with money are budgets

24. Of the following, the one which is NOT a contribution that a budget makes to organizational programming is that a budget

    A. enables a comparison of what actually happened with what was expected
    B. stresses the need to forecast specific goals and eliminates the need to focus on tasks needed to accomplish goals
    C. may illustrate duplication of effort between interdependent activities
    D. shows the relationship between various organizational segments

25. A line-item budget is a good control budget because

    A. it clearly specifies how the items being purchased will be used
    B. expenditures can be shown primarily for contractual services
    C. it clearly specifies what the money is buying
    D. it clearly specifies the services to be provided

KEY (CORRECT ANSWERS)

1.	B	11.	B
2.	C	12.	B
3.	A	13.	C
4.	B	14.	B
5.	B	15.	D
6.	A	16.	A
7.	A	17.	D
8.	D	18.	C
9.	D	19.	D
10.	B	20.	B

21. C
22. D
23. C
24. B
25. C

TEST 2

DIRECTIONS: Each question or incomplete statement is followed by several suggested answers or completions. Select the one that BEST answers the question or completes the statement. *PRINT THE LETTER OF THE CORRECT ANSWER IN THE SPACE AT THE RIGHT.*

1. The insights of Chester I. Barnard have influenced the development of management thought in significant ways. He is MOST closely identified with a position that has become known as the

    A. acceptance theory of authority
    B. principle of the manager's or executive's span of control
    C. *Theory X* and *Theory Y* dichotomy
    D. unit of command principle

    1.____

2. Certain conditions should exist to insure that a subordinate will decide to accept a communication as being authoritative.
   Which of the following is LEAST valid as a condition which should exist?

    A. The subordinate understands the communication.
    B. At the time of the subordinate's decision, he views the communication as consistent with the organization's purpose and his personal interest.
    C. At the time of the subordinate's decision, he views the communication as more consistent with his personal purposes than with the organization's interest.
    D. The subordinate is mentally and physically able to comply with the communication.

    2.____

3. In exploring the effects that employee participation has on implementing changes in work methods, certain relationships have been established between participation and productivity.
   It has MOST generally been found that highest productivity occurs in groups provided with

    A. participation in the process of change only through representatives of their group
    B. no participation in the change process
    C. full participation in the change process
    D. intermittent participation in the process of change

    3.____

4. The trend LEAST likely to occur in the area of employee-management relations is that

    A. employees will exert more influence on decisions affecting their interests
    B. technological change will have a stronger impact on organizations' human resources
    C. labor will judge management according to company profits
    D. government will play a larger role in balancing the interests of the parties in labor-management affairs

    4.____

5. Members of an organization must satisfy several fundamental psychological needs in order to be happy and productive.
   The BROADEST and MOST basic needs are

   A. achievement, recognition, and acceptance
   B. competition, recognition, and accomplishment
   C. salary increments and recognition
   D. acceptance of competition and economic award

6. Morale has been defined as the capacity of a group of people to pull together steadily for a common purpose.
   Morale thus defined is MOST generally dependent on

   A. job security
   B. group and individual self-confidence
   C. organizational efficiency
   D. physical health of the individuals

7. Which is the CORRECT order of steps to follow when revising office procedure?
   To

   I. develop the improved method as determined by time and motion studies and effective workplace layout
   II. find out how the task is now performed
   III. apply the new method
   IV. analyze the current method

   The CORRECT answer is:
   A. IV, II, I, III   B. II, I, III, IV
   C. I, II, IV, III   D. II, IV, I, III

8. In contrast to broad spans of control, narrow spans of control are MOST likely to

   A. provide opportunity for more personal contact between superior and subordinate
   B. encourage decentralization
   C. stress individual initiative
   D. foster group of team effort

9. A manager is coaching a subordinate on the nature of decision-making.
   She could BEST define decision-making as

   A. choosing between alternatives
   B. making diagnoses of feasible ends
   C. making diagnoses of feasible means
   D. comparing alternatives

10. Of the following, the LEAST valid purpose of an organizational policy statement is to

    A. keep personnel from performing improper actions and functions on routine matters
    B. prevent the mishandling of non-routine matters
    C. provide management personnel with a tool that precludes the need for their use of judgment
    D. provide standard decisions and approaches in handling problems of a recurrent nature

11. Current thinking on bureaucratic organizations is that

    A. bureaucracy is on the way out
    B. bureaucracy, though not perfect, is unlikely to be replaced
    C. bureaucratic organizations are most effective in dealing with constant change
    D. bureaucratic organizations are most effective when dealing with sophisticated customers or clients

12. The development of alternate plans as a major step in planning will normally result in the planner's having several possible course of action available. GENERALLY, this is

    A. *desirable* since such development helps to determine the most suitable alternative and to provide for the unexpected
    B. *desirable* since such development makes the use of planning premises and constraints unnecessary
    C. *undesirable* since the planners should formulate only one way of achieving given goals at a given time
    D. *undesirable* since such action restricts efforts to modify the planning to take advantage of opportunities

13. Assume a manager carries out his responsibilities to his staff according to what is now known about managerial leadership.
    Which of the following statements would MOST accurately reflect his assumptions about proper management?

    A. Efficiency in operations results from allowing the human element to participate in a minimal way.
    B. Efficient operation results from balancing work considerations with personnel considerations.
    C. Efficient operation results from a work force committed to its self-interest.
    D. Efficient operation results from staff relationships that produce a friendly work climate.

14. Assume that a manager is called upon to conduct a management audit. To do this properly, he would have to take certain steps in a specific sequence. Which step should this manager take FIRST?

    A. Managerial performance must be surveyed.
    B. A method of reporting must be established.
    C. Management auditing procedures and documentation must be developed.
    D. Criteria for the audit must be established.

15. If a manager is required to conduct a scientific investigation of an organizational problem, the FIRST step he should take is to

    A. state his assumptions about the problem
    B. carry out a search for background information
    C. choose the right approach to investigate the validity of his assumptions
    D. define and state the problem

16. A manager would be correct to assert that the principle of delegation states that decisions should be made PRIMARILY

    A. by persons in an executive capacity qualified to make them
    B. by persons in a non-executive capacity
    C. at as low an organizational level of authority as practicable
    D. by the next lower level of authority

17. Of the following, which one is NOT regarded by management authorities as a fundamental characteristic of an ideal bureaucracy?

    A. Division of labor and specialization
    B. An established hierarchy
    C. Decentralization of authority
    D. A set of operating rules and regulations

18. As the number of subordinates in a manager's span of control increases, the actual number of possible relationships

    A. increases disproportionately to the number of subordinates
    B. increases in equal number to the number of subordinates
    C. reaches a stable level
    D. will first increase, then slowly decrease

19. Management experts generally believe that computer-based management information systems (MIS) have greater potential for improving the process of management than any other development in recent decades.
The one of the following which MOST accurately describes the objectives of MIS is to

   A. provide information for decision-making on planning, initiating, and controlling the operations of the various units of the organization
   B. establish mechanization of routine functions such as clerical records, payroll, inventory, and accounts receivable in order to promote economy and efficiency
   C. computerize decision-making on planning, initiating, organizing, and controlling the operations of an organization
   D. provide accurate facts and figures on the various programs of the organization to be used for purposes of planning and research

20. The one of the following which is the BEST application of the *management-by-exception* principle is that this principle

   A. stimulates communication and aids in management of crisis situations, thus reducing the frequency of decision-making
   B. saves time and reserves top management decisions only for crisis situations, thus reducing the frequency of decision-making
   C. stimulates communication, saves time, and reduces the frequency of decision-making
   D. is limited to crisis-management situations

21. Generally, each organization is dependent upon the availability of qualified personnel.
Of the following, the MOST important factor affecting the availability of qualified people to each organization is

   A. availability of public transportation
   B. the general rise in the educational levels of our population
   C. the rise of sentiment against racial discrimination
   D. pressure by organized community groups

22. A fundamental responsibility of all managers is to decide what physical facilities and equipment are needed to help attain basic goals.
Good planning for the purchase and use of equipment is seldom easy to do and is complicated most by the fact that

   A. organizations rarely have stable sources of supply
   B. nearly all managers tend to be better at personnel planning than at equipment planning
   C. decisions concerning physical resources are made too often on an emergency basis rather than under carefully prepared policies
   D. legal rulings relative to depreciation fluctuate very frequently

23. In attempting to reconcile managerial objectives and an individual employee's goals, it is generally LEAST desirable for management to

    A. recognize the capacity of the individual to contribute toward realization of managerial goals
    B. encourage self-development of the employee to exceed minimum job performance
    C. consider an individual employee's work separately from other employees
    D. demonstrate that an employee advances only to the extent that he contributes directly to the accomplishment of stated goals

23.____

24. As a management tool for discovering individual training needs, a job analysis would generally be of LEAST assistance in determining

    A. the performance requirements of individual jobs
    B. actual employee performance on the job
    C. acceptable standards of performance
    D. training needs for individual jobs

24.____

25. One of the major concerns of organizational managers today is how the spread of automation will affect them and the status of their positions. Realistically speaking, one can say that the MOST likely effect of our newer forms of highly automated technology on managers will be to

    A. make most top-level positions superfluous or obsolete
    B. reduce the importance of managerial work in general
    C. replace the work of managers with the work of technicians
    D. increase the importance of and demand for top managerial personnel

25.____

KEY (CORRECT ANSWERS)

1. A		11. B	
2. C		12. A	
3. C		13. B	
4. C		14. D	
5. A		15. D	
6. B		16. C	
7. D		17. C	
8. A		18. A	
9. A		19. A	
10. C		20. C	

21. B
22. C
23. C
24. B
25. D

EXAMINATION SECTION
TEST 1

DIRECTIONS: Each question or incomplete statement is followed by several suggested answers or completions. Select the one that BEST answers the question or completes the statement. *PRINT THE LETTER OF THE CORRECT ANSWER IN THE SPACE AT THE RIGHT.*

1. A management approach widely used today is based on the belief that decisions should be made and actions should be taken by managers closest to the organization's problems.
    This style of management is MOST appropriately called _____ management.
    A. scientific
    B. means-end
    C. decentralized
    D. internal process

    1._____

2. As contrasted with tall organization structures with narrow spans of control, flat organization structures with wide spans of control MOST usually provide
    A. fast communication and information flows
    B. more levels in the organizational hierarchy
    C. fewer workers reporting to supervisors
    D. lower motivation because of tighter control standards

    2._____

3. Use of the systems approach is MOST likely to lead to
    A. consideration of the impact on the whole organization of actions taken in any part of that organization
    B. the placing of restrictions on departmental activity
    C. use of mathematical models to suboptimize production
    D. consideration of the activities of each unit of an organization as a totality without regard to the remainder of the organization

    3._____

4. An administrator, with overall responsibility for all administrative operations in a large operating agency, is considering organizing the agency's personnel office around either of the following two alternative concepts:
    Alternative I: A corps of specialists for each branch of personnel subject matter, whose skills, counsel, or work products are coordinated only by the agency personnel officer
    Alternative II: A crew of so-called *personnel generalists*, who individually work with particular segments of the organization but deal with all subspecialties of the personnel function
    The one of the following which MOST tends to be a DRAWBACK of Alternative I, as compared with Alternative II, is that
    A. training and employee relations work call for education, interests, and talents that differ from those required for classification and compensation work
    B. personnel office staff may develop only superficial familiarity with the specialized areas to which they have been assigned

    4._____

C. supervisors may fail to get continuing overall personnel advice on an integrated basis
D. the personnel specialists are likely to become so interested in and identified with the operating view as to particular cases that they lose their professional objectivity and become merely advocates of what some supervisor wants

5. The matrix summary or decision matrix is a useful tool for making choices. Its effectiveness is MOST dependent upon the user's ability to
    A. write a computer program (Fortran or Cobol)
    B. assign weights representing the relative importance of the objectives
    C. solve a set of two equations with two unknowns
    D. work with matrix algebra

6. An organizational form which is set up only on an *ad hoc* basis to meet specific goals is said PRIMARILY to use
    A. clean break departmentation
    B. matrix or task force organization
    C. scalar specialization
    D. geographic or area-wide decentralization

7. The concept of job enlargement would LEAST properly be implemented by
    A. permitting workers to follow through on tasks or projects from start to finish
    B. delegating the maximum authority possible for decision-making to lower levels in the hierarchy
    C. maximizing the number of professional classes in the classification plan
    D. training employees to grow beyond whatever tasks they have been performing

8. As used in the area of admission, the principle of *unity of command* MOST specifically means that
    A. an individual should report to only one superior for any single activity
    B. individuals make better decisions than do committees
    C. in large organizations, chains of command are normally too long
    D. an individual should not supervise over five subordinates

9. The method of operations research, statistical decision-making, and linear programming have been referred to as the tool kit of the manager. Utilization of these tools is LEAST useful in the performance of which of the following functions?
    A. Elimination of the need for using judgment when making decisions
    B. Facilitation of decision-making without the need for sub-optimization
    C. Quantifying problems for management study
    D. Research and analysis of management operations

10. When acting in their respective managerial capacities, the chief executive officer and the office supervisor both perform the fundamental functions of management.
    Of the following differences between the two, the one which is generally considered to be the LEAST significant is the
    A. breadth of the objectives
    B. complexity of measuring actual efficiency of performance
    C. number of decisions made
    D. organizational relationships affected by actions taken

11. The ability of operations researchers to solve complicated problems rests on their use of models.
    These models can BEST be described as
    A. mathematical statements of the problem
    B. physical constructs that simulate a work layout
    C. toy-like representations of employees in work environments
    D. role-playing simulations

12. Of the following, it is MOST likely to be proper for the agency head to allow the agency personnel officer to make final selection of appointees from certified eligible lists where there are
    A. *small* numbers of employees to be hired in newly-developed professional fields
    B. *large* numbers of persons to be hired for key managerial positions
    C. *large* numbers of persons to be hired in very routine occupations where the individual discretion of operating officials is not vital
    D. *small* numbers of persons to be hired in highly specialized professional occupations which are vital to the agency's operations

13. Of the following, an operating agency personnel office is LEAST likely to be able to exert strong influence or control within the operating agency by
    A. interpreting to the operating agency head what is intended by the directives and rules emanating from the central personnel agency
    B. establishing the key objectives of those line divisions of the operating agency employing large numbers of staff and operating under the management-by-objectives approach
    C. formulating and proposing to the agency head the internal policies and procedures on personnel matters required within the operating agency
    D. exercising certain discretionary authority in the application of the agency head's general personnel policies to actual specific situations

14. PERT is a recently developed system used PRIMARILY to
    A. evaluate the quality of applicants' background
    B. analyze and control the timing aspects of a major project
    C. control the total expenditure of agency funds within a monthly or quarterly time period
    D. analyze and control the differential effect on costs of purchasing different quantities

15. Assume that an operating agency has among its vacant positions two positions, each of which encompasses mixed duties. Both require appointees to have considerable education and experience, but these requirements are essential only for the more difficult duties of these positions. In the place of these positions, an administrator creates two new positions, one in which the higher duties are concentrated and the other with the lesser functions requiring only minimum preparation.
Of the following, it is generally MOST appropriate to characterize the administrator's action as a(n)
    A. *undesirable* example of deliberate downgrading of standards and requirements
    B. *undesirable* manipulation of the classification system for non-merit purposes
    C. *desirable* broadening of the definition of a class of positions
    D. *desirable* example of job redesign

16. Of the following, the LEAST important stumbling block to the development of personnel mobility among governmental jurisdictions is the
    A. limitations on lateral entry above junior levels in many jurisdictions
    B. continued collection of filing fees for civil service tests by many governmental jurisdictions
    C. absence of reciprocal exchange of retirement benefit eligibility between governments
    D. disparities in salary scales between governments

17. Of the following, the MAJOR disadvantage of a personnel system that features the *selection out* (forced retirement) of those who have been passed over a number of times for promotion is that such a system
    A. wastes manpower which is perfectly competent at one level but unable to rise above that level
    B. wastes funds by requiring review boards
    C. leads to excessive recruiting of newcomers from outside the system
    D. may not be utilized in *closed* career systems with low maximum age limits for entrance

18. Of the following, the fields in which operating agency personnel offices generally exercise the MOST stringent controls over first line supervisors in the agency are
    A. methods analysis and work simplification
    B. selection and position classification
    C. vestibule training and Gantt chart
    D. suggestion systems and staff development

19. Of the following, computers are normally MOST effective in handling
    A. large masses of data requiring simple processing
    B. small amounts of data requiring constantly changing complex processing
    C. data for which reported values are often subject to inaccuracies
    D. large amounts of data requiring continual programming and reprocessing

20. Contingency planning, which has long been used by the military and is assuming increasing importance in other organizations, may BEST be described as a process which utilizes
    A. alternative plans based on varying assumptions
    B. *crash programs* by organizations departmentalized along process lines
    C. plans which mandate substitution of equipment for manpower at predetermined operational levels
    D. plans that individually and accurately predict future events

21. In the management of inventory, two kinds of costs normally determine when to order and in what amounts.
    The one of the following choices which includes BOTH of these kinds of costs is _____ costs and _____ costs.
    A. carrying; storage
    B. personnel; order
    C. computer; order
    D. personnel; computer

22. At top management levels, the one of the following which is generally the MOST important executive skill is skill in
    A. budgeting procedures
    B. a technical discipline
    C. controlling actions in accordance with previously approved plans
    D. seeing the organization as a whole

23. Of the following, the BEST way to facilitate the successful operation of a committee is to set guidelines establishing its
    A. budget exclusive of personnel costs
    B. location
    C. schedule of meetings or conferences
    D. scope of purpose

24. Executive training programs that single out particular managers and groom them for promotion create the so-called organizational *crown princes*.
    Of the following, the MOST serious problem that arises in connection with this practice is that
    A. the managers chosen for promotion seldom turn out to be the best managers since the future potential of persons cannot be predicted
    B. not enough effort is made to remove organizational obstacles in the way of their development and achievement
    C. the resentment of the managers not selected for the program has an adverse effect on the motivation of those managers not selected
    D. performance appraisal and review are not carried out systematically enough

25. Of the following, the LEAST likely result of the use of the concept of job enlargement is that
    A. coordination will be simplified
    B. the individual's job will become less challenging
    C. worker satisfaction will increase
    D. fewer people will have to give attention to each piece of work

KEY (CORRECT ANSWERS)

1.	C	11.	A
2.	A	12.	C
3.	A	13.	B
4.	C	14.	B
5.	B	15.	D
6.	B	16.	B
7.	C	17.	A
8.	A	18.	B
9.	A	19.	A
10.	C	20.	A

21. A
22. D
23. D
24. C
25. B

TEST 2

DIRECTIONS: Each question or incomplete statement is followed by several suggested answers or completions. Select the one that BEST answers the question or completes the statement. *PRINT THE LETTER OF THE CORRECT ANSWER IN THE SPACE AT THE RIGHT.*

1. The one of the following which is MOST likely to be emphasized in the use of the brainstorming technique is the
    A. early consideration of cost factors of all ideas which may be suggested
    B. avoidance of impractical suggestions
    C. separation of the generation of ideas from their evaluation
    D. appraisal of suggestions concurrently with their initial presentation

1.____

2. Of the following, the BEST method for assessing managerial performance is generally to
    A. compare the manager's accomplishments against clear, specific, agreed-upon goals
    B. compare the manager's traits with those of his peers on a predetermined objective
    C. measure the manager's behavior against a listing of itemized personal traits
    D. measure the manager's success according to the enumeration of the *satisfaction* principle

2.____

3. As compared with recruitment from outside, selection from within the service must generally show GREATER concern for the
    A. prestige in which the public service as a whole is held by the public
    B. morale of the candidate group compromising the recruitment field
    C. cost of examining per candidate
    D. benefits of the use of standardized and validated tests

3.____

4. Performance budgeting focuses PRIMARY attention upon which one of the following? The
    A. things to be acquired, such as supplies and equipment
    B. general character and relative importance of the work to be done or the service to be rendered
    C. list of personnel to be employed, by specific title
    D. separation of employee performance evaluations from employee compensation

4.____

5. Of the following, the FIRST step in the installation and operation of a performance budgeting system generally should be the
    A. identification of program costs in relationship to the accounting system and operating structure
    B. identification of the specific end results of past programs in other jurisdictions

5.____

C. identification of work programs that are meaningful for management purposes
D. establishment of organizational structures each containing only one work program

6. Of the following, the MOST important purpose of a system of quarterly allotments of appropriated funds generally is to enable the
   A. head of the judicial branch to determine the legality of agency requests for budget increases
   B. operating agencies of government to upgrade the quality of their services without increasing costs
   C. head of the executive branch to control the rate at which the operating agencies obligate and expend funds
   D. operating agencies of government to avoid payment for services which have not been properly rendered by employees

7. In the preparation of the agency's budget, the agency's central budget office has two responsibilities: program review and management improvement. Which one of the following questions concerning an operating agency's program is MOST closely related to the agency budget officer's program review responsibility?
   A. Can expenditures for supplies, materials, or equipment be reduced?
   B. Will improved work methods contribute to a more effective program?
   C. What is the relative importance of this program as compared to a higher level of program performance?
   D. Will a realignment of responsibilities contribute to a higher level of program performance?

8. Of the following, the method of evaluating relative rates of return normally and generally thought to be MOST useful in evaluating government operations is _____ analysis.
   A. cost-benefit   B. budget variance
   C. investment capital   D. budget planning program

9. The one of the following assumptions that is LEAST likely to be made by a democratic or permissive type of leader is that
   A. commitment to goals is seldom a result of monetary rewards alone
   B. people can learn not only to accept, but also to seek, responsibility
   C. the average person prefers security over advancement
   D. creativity may be found in most segments of the population

10. In attempting to motivate subordinates, a manager should PRINCIPALLY be aware of the fact that
    A. the psychological qualities of people, in general, are easily predictable
    B. fear, as a traditional form of motivation, has lost much of its former power to motivate people in our modern industrial society
    C. fear is still the most potent force in motivating the behavior of subordinates in the public service
    D. the worker has very little control over the quality and quantity of his output

11. Assume that the following figures represent the number of work-unit that were produced during a week by each of sixteen employees in a division:

    12 16 13 18
    21 12 16 13
    16 13 17 21
    13 15 18 20

    If all of the employees of the division who produced thirteen work-units during the week had instead produced fifteen work-units during that same week, then for that week the
    A. mean, median, and mode would all change
    B. mean and mode would change, but the median would remain the same
    C. mode and median would change, but the mean would remain the same
    D. mode, mean, and median would all still remain unchanged in value

12. An important law in motivation theory is called the *law of effect*. This law says that behavior which satisfies a person's needs tends to be repeated; behavior which does not satisfy a person's needs tends to be eliminated.
    The one of the following which is the BEST interpretation of this law is that
    A. productivity depends on personality traits
    B. diversity of goals leads to instability and motivation
    C. the greater the satisfaction, the more likely it is that the behavior will be reinforced
    D. extrinsic satisfaction is more important than intrinsic reward

13. Of the following, the MOST acceptable reason an administrator can give for taking advice from other employees in the organization only when he asks for it is that he wants to
    A. encourage creativity and high morale
    B. keep dysfunctional pressures and inconsistent recommendations to a minimum
    C. show his superiors and peers who is in charge
    D. show his subordinates who is in charge

14. A complete picture of the communication channels in an organization can BEST be revealed by
    A. observing the planned paperwork system
    B. recording the highly intermittent patterns of communication
    C. plotting the entire flow of information over a period of time
    D. monitoring the *grapevine*

Questions 15-16.

DIRECTIONS: Questions 15 and 16 are to be answered SOLELY on the basis of the following passage.

Management by objectives (MBO) may be defined as the process by which the superior and the subordinate managers of an organization jointly define its common goals, define each individual's major areas of responsibility in terms of the results expected of him and use these measures as guides for operating the unit and assessing the contribution of each of its members.

The MBO approach requires that after organizational goals are established and communicated, targets must be set for each individual position which are congruent with organizational goals. Periodic performance reviews and a final review using the objectives set as criteria are also basic to this approach.

Recent studies have shown that MBO programs are influenced by attitudes and perceptions of the boss, the company, the reward-punishment system, and the program itself. In addition, the manner in which the MBO program is carried out can influence the success of the program. A study done in the late sixties indicates that the best results are obtained when the manager sets goals which deal with significant problem areas in the organizational unit, or with the subordinate's personal deficiencies. These goals must be clear with regard to what is expected of the subordinate. The frequency of feedback is also important in the success of a management-by-objectives program. Generally, the greater the amount of feedback, the more successful the MBO program.

15. According to the above passage, the expected output for individual employees should be determined
    A. after a number of reviews of work performance
    B. after common organizational goals are defined
    C. before common organizational goals are defined
    D. on the basis of an employee's personal qualities

15.____

16. According to the above passage, the management-by-objectives approach requires
    A. less feedback than other types of management programs
    B. little review of on-the-job performance after the initial setting of goals
    C. general conformance between individual goals and organizational goals
    D. the setting of goals which deal with minor problem area in the organization

16.____

Questions 17-19.

DIRECTIONS: Questions 17 through 19 are to be answered SOLELY on the basis of the following passage.

During the last decade, a great deal of interest has been generated around the phenomenon of organizational development, or the process of developing human resources through conscious organization effort. Organizational development (OD) stresses improving interpersonal relationships and organizational skills, such as communication, to a much greater degree than individual training ever did.

The kind of training that an organization should emphasize depends upon the present and future structure of the organization. If future organizations are to be unstable, shifting coalitions, then individual skills and abilities, particularly those emphasizing innovativeness, creativity, flexibility, and the latest technological knowledge, are crucial, and individual training is most appropriate.

But if there is to be little change in organizational structure, then the main thrust of training should be group-oriented or organizational development. This approach seems better designed for overcoming hierarchical barriers, for developing a degree of interpersonal relationships which make communication along the chain of command possible, and for retaining a modicum of innovation and/or flexibility.

17. According to the above passage, group-oriented training is MOST useful in
    A. developing a communications system that will facilitate understanding through the chain of command
    B. highly flexible and mobile organizations
    C. preventing the crossing of hierarchical barriers within an organization
    D. saving energy otherwise wasted on developing methods of dealing with rigid hierarchies

17.____

18. The one of the following conclusions which can be drawn MOST appropriately from the above passage is that
    A. behavioral research supports the use of organizational development training method rather than individualized training
    B. it is easier to provide individualized training in specific skills than to set up sensitivity training programs
    C. organizational development eliminates innovative or flexible activity
    D. the nature of an organization greatly influences which training methods will be most effective

18.____

19. According to the above passage, the one of the following which is LEAST important for large-scale organizations geared to rapid and abrupt change is
    A. current technological information
    B. development of a high degree of interpersonal relationships
    C. development of individual skills and abilities
    D. emphasis on creativity

19.____

Questions 20-25.

DIRECTIONS: Each of Questions 20 through 25 consist of a statement which contains one word that is incorrectly used because it is not in keeping with the meaning that the quotation is evidently intended to convey. Determine which word is INCORRECTLY used. Select from the choices lettered A, B, C, and D the word which, when substituted for the incorrectly used word, would BEST help to convey the meaning of the statement.

20. One of the considerations likely to affect the currency of classification, particularly in professional and managerial occupations, is the impact of the incumbent's capacities on the job. Some work is highly susceptible to change as the result of the special talents or interests of the classifier. Organization should never be so rigid as not to capitalize on the innovative or unusual proclivities of its key employees. While a machine operator may not be able, even subtly, to change the character or level of his job, the design engineer, the attorney, or the organization and methods analyst might readily do so. Reliance on his judgment and the scope of his assignments may both grow as the result of his skill, insight, and capacity.
   A. unlikely   B. incumbent   C. directly   D. scope

20.____

21. The supply of services by the state is not governed by market price. The aim is to supply such services to all who need them and to treat all consumers equally. This objective especially compels the civil servant to maintain a role f strict impartiality, based on the principle of equality of individual citizens vis-à-vis their government. However, there is a clear difference between being neutral and impartial. If the requirement is construed to mean that all civil servants should be political eunuchs, devoid of the drive and motivation essential to dynamic administration, then the concept of impartiality is being seriously utilized. Modern governments should not be stopped from demanding that their hirelings have not only the technical but the emotional qualifications necessary for whole-hearted effort.
   A. determined   B. rule   C. stable   D. misapplied

21.____

22. The manager was barely listening. Recently, at the divisional level, several new fronts of troubles had erupted, including a requirement to increase production yet hold down operating costs and somehow raise quality standards. Though the three objectives were basically obsolete, top departmental management was insisting on the simultaneous attainment of them, an insistence not helping the manager's ulcer, an old enemy within. Thus, the manager could not find time for interest in individuals—only in statistics which regiment of individuals, like unconsidered Army privates, added up to.
   A. quantity   B. battalion   C. incompatible   D. quiet

22.____

23. When a large volume of data flows directly between operators and first-line supervisors, senior executives tend to be out of the mainstream of work. Summary reports can increase their remoteness. An executive needs to know the volume, quality, and cost of completed work, and exceptional problems. In addition, he may desire information on key operating conditions. Summary reports on these matters are, therefore, essential features of a communications network and make delegation without loss of control possible.
   A. unimportant   B. quantity   C. offset   D. incomplete

23.____

24. Of major significance in management is harmony between the overall objectives of the organization and the managerial objectives within that organization. In addition, harmony among goals of managers is impossible; they should not be at cross-purposes. Each manager's goal should supplement and assist the goals of his colleagues. Likewise, the objectives of individuals or non-management members should be harmonized with those of the manager. When this is accomplished, genuine teamwork is the result, and human relations are aided materially. The integration of managers' and individuals' goals aids in achieving greater work satisfaction at all levels.
    A. competition   B. dominate   C. incremental   D. vital

    24.____

25. Change constantly challenges the manager. Some of this change is evolutionary, some revolutionary, some recognizable, some non-recognizable. Both forces within an enterprise and forces outside the enterprise cause managers to act and react in initiating changes in their immediate working environment. Change invalidates existing operations. Goals are not being accomplished in the best manner, problems develop, and frequently because of the lack of time, only patched-up solutions are followed. The result is that the mode of management is profound in nature and temporary in effectiveness. A complete overhaul of managerial operations should take place. It appears quite likely that we are just beginning to see the real effects of change in our society; the pace probably will accelerate in ways that few really understand or know how to handle.
    A. confirms   B. decline   C. instituting   D. superficial

    25.____

KEY (CORRECT ANSWERS)

1.	C		11.	B
2.	A		12.	C
3.	B		13.	B
4.	B		14.	C
5.	C		15.	B
6.	C		16.	C
7.	C		17.	A
8.	A		18.	D
9.	C		19.	B
10.	B		20.	B

21.	D
22.	C
23.	C
24.	D
25.	D

EXAMINATION SECTION
TEST 1

DIRECTIONS: Each question or incomplete statement is followed by several suggested answers or completions. Select the one that BEST answers the question or completes the statement. *PRINT THE LETTER OF THE CORRECT ANSWER IN THE SPACE AT THE RIGHT.*

1. Assume that a manager is preparing a list of reasons to justify making a major change in methods and procedures in his agency.
   Which of the following reasons would be LEAST appropriate on such a list?
   A. Improve the means for satisfying needs and wants of agency personnel
   B. Increase efficiency
   C. Intensify competition and stimulate loyalty to separate work groups
   D. Contribute to the individual and group satisfaction of agency personnel

    1.____

2. Many managers recognize the benefits of decentralization but are concerned about the danger of over-relaxation of control as a result of increased delegation.
   Of the following, the MOST appropriate means of establishing proper control under decentralization is for the manager to
   A. establish detailed standards for all phases of operation
   B. shift his attention from operating details to appraisal of results
   C. keep himself informed by decreasing the time span covered by reports
   D. make unilateral decisions on difficult situations that arise in decentralized locations

    2.____

3. In some agencies, the counsel to the agency head is given the right to bypass the chain of command and issue orders directly to the staff concerning matters that involve certain specific processes and practices.
   This situation MOST NEARLY illustrates the principle of _____ authority.
   A. the acceptance theory of   B. multiple-linear
   C. splintered   D. functional

    3.____

4. Assume that a manager is writing a brief report to his superior outlining the advantages of matrix organization.
   Of the following, it would be INCORRECT to state that
   A. in matrix organization, a project is emphasized by designating one individual as the focal point for all matters pertaining to it
   B. utilization of manpower can be flexible in matrix organization because a reservoir of specialists is maintained in the line operations
   C. the usual line staff arrangement is generally reversed in matrix organization
   D. in matrix organization, responsiveness to project needs is generally faster due to establishing needed communication lines and decision points

    4.____

5. It is commonly understood that communication is an important part of the administrative process.
   Which of the following is NOT a valid principle of the communication process in administration?
   A. The channels of communication should be spontaneous.
   B. The lines of communication should be as direct and as short as possible.
   C. Communications should be authenticated.
   D. The persons serving in communications centers should be competent.

6. The PRIMARY purpose of the quantitative approach in management is to
   A. identify better alternatives for management decision-making
   B. substitute data for judgment
   C. match opinions to data
   D. match data to opinions

7. If an executive wants to make a strong case for running his agency as a flat type of structure, he should point out that the PRIMARY advantage of doing so is to
   A. provide less experience in decision-making for agency personnel
   B. facilitate frequent contact between each superior and his immediate subordinates
   C. improve communication and unify attitudes
   D. improve communication and diversify attitudes

8. In deciding how detailed his delegation of authority to a subordinate should be, a manager should follow the general principle that
   A. delegation of authority is more detailed at the top of the organizational structure
   B. detailed delegation of authority is associated with detailed work assignments
   C. delegation of authority should be in sufficient detail to prevent overlapping assignments
   D. detailed delegation of authority is associated with broad work assignments

9. In recent years, newer and more fluid types of organizational forms have been developed. One of these is a type of free-form organization.
   Another name for this type of organization is the
   A. project organization   B. semimix organization
   C. naturalistic structure   D. semipermanent structure

10. Which of the following is the MAJOR objective of operational or management systems audits?
    A. Determining the number of personnel needed
    B. Recommending opportunities for improving operating and management practices
    C. Detecting fraud
    D. Determining organization problems

11. Assume that a manager observes that conflict exists between his agency and another operating agency of government.
    Which of the following statements is the LEAST probable cause of this conflict?
    A. Incompatibility between the agencies' goals but similarity in their resource allocations
    B. Compatibility between agencies' goals and resources
    C. Status differences between agency personnel
    D. Differences in perceptions of each other's policies

12. Of the following, a MAJOR purpose of brainstorming as a problem-solving technique is to
    A. develop the ability to concentrate
    B. encourage creative thinking
    C. evaluate employees' ideas
    D. develop critical ability

13. The one of the following requirements which is LEAST likely to accompany regular delegation of work from a manager to a subordinate is a(n)
    A. need to review the organization's workload
    B. indication of what work the subordinate is to do
    C. need to grant authority to the subordinate
    D. obligation for the subordinate who accepts the work to try to complete it

14. Of the following, the one factor which is generally considered LEAST essential to successful committee operation is
    A. stating a clear definition of the authority and scope of the committee
    B. selecting the committee chairman carefully
    C. limiting the size of the committee to four persons
    D. limiting the subject matter to that which can be handled in group discussion

15. In using the program evaluation and review technique, the *critical path* is the path that
    A. requires the shortest time
    B. requires the longest time
    C. focuses most attention on social constraints
    D. focuses most attention to repetitious jobs

16. Which one of the following is LEAST characteristic of the management-by-objectives approach?
    A. The scope within which the employee may exercise decision-making is broadened.
    B. The employee starts with a self-appraisal of his performances, abilities, and potential.
    C. Emphasis is placed on activities performed; activities orientation is maximized.
    D. Each employee participates in determining his own objectives.

17. The function of management which puts into effect the decisions, plans, and programs that have previously been worked out for achieving the goals of the group is MOST appropriately called
    A. scheduling   B. classifying   C. budgeting   D. directing

18. In the establishment of a plan to improve office productive efficiency, which of the following guidelines is LEAST helpful in setting sound work standards?
    A. Employees must accept the plan's objectives.
    B. Current production averages must be promulgated as work standards for a group.
    C. The work flow must generally be fairly constant.
    D. The operation of the plan must be expressed in terms understandable to the worker.

19. The one of the following activities which, generally speaking, is of *relatively* MAJOR importance at the lower-management level and of *somewhat* LESSER importance at higher-management levels is
    A. actuating   B. forecasting   C. organizing   D. planning

20. Three styles of leadership exist: democratic, authoritarian, and laissez-faire. Of the following work situations, the one in which a democratic approach would normally be the MOST effective is when the work is
    A. routine and moderately complex   B. repetitious and simple
    C. complex and not routine   D. simple and not routine

21. Governmental and business organizations *generally* encounter the GREATEST difficulties in developing tangible measures of which one of the following?
    A. The level of expenditures   B. Contributions to social welfare
    C. Retention rates   D. Causes of labor unrest

22. Of the following, a *management-by-objectives* program is BEST described as
    A. a new comprehensive plan of organization
    B. introduction of budgets and financial controls
    C. introduction of long-range planning
    D. development of future goals with supporting and related progress reviews

23. Research and analysis is probably the most widely used technique for selecting alternatives when major planning decisions are involved.
    Of the following, a VALUABLE characteristic of research and analysis is that this technique
    A. places the problem in a meaningful conceptual framework
    B. involves practical application of the various alternatives
    C. accurately analyzes all important tangibles
    D. is much less expensive than other problem-solving methods

24. If a manager were assigned the task of using a systems approach to designing a new work unit, which of the following should he consider FIRST in carrying out his design?
    A. Networks
    B. Work flows and information processes
    C. Linkages and relationships
    D. Decision points and control loops

25. The MAIN distinction between Theory X and Theory Y approaches to organization, in accordance with Douglas McGregor's view, is that Theory Y
    A. considers that work is natural to people; Theory X assumes that people are lazy and avoid work
    B. leads to a tall, narrow organization structure, while Theory X leads to one that is flat
    C. organizations motivate people with money; Theory X organizations motivate people with good working conditions
    D. represents authoritarian management, while Theory X management is participative

KEY (CORRECT ANSWERS)

1.	C		11.	B
2.	B		12.	B
3.	D		13.	A
4.	C		14.	C
5.	A		15.	B
6.	A		16.	C
7.	C		17.	D
8.	B		18.	B
9.	A		19.	A
10.	B		20.	C

21.	B
22.	D
23.	A
24.	B
25.	A

TEST 2

DIRECTIONS: Each question or incomplete statement is followed by several suggested answers or completions. Select the one that BEST answers the question or completes the statement. *PRINT THE LETTER OF THE CORRECT ANSWER IN THE SPACE AT THE RIGHT.*

1. Of the following, the stage in decision-making which is usually MOST difficult is
   A. stating the alternatives
   B. predicting the possible outcome of each alternative
   C. evaluating the relative merits of each alternative
   D. minimizing the undesirable aspects of the alternative selected

   1.____

2. In a department where a clerk is reporting both to a senior clerk in charge of the mail room and also to a supervising clerk in charge of the duplicating section, there may be a breakdown of the management principle called
   A. horizontal specialization   B. job enrichment
   C. unity of command   D. Graicunas' Law

   2.____

3. Of the following, the failure by line managers to accept and appreciate the benefits and limitations of a new program or system VERY frequently can be traced to the
   A. budgetary problems involved
   B. resultant need to reduce staff
   C. lack of controls it engenders
   D. failure of top management to support its implementation

   3.____

4. Although there is general agreement that *management-by-objectives* has made a major contribution to modern management of large organizations, criticisms of the system during the past few years have resulted in
   A. mounting pressure for relaxation of management goals
   B. renewed concern with human values and the manager's personal needs
   C. over-mechanistic application of the perceptions of the behavioral scientists
   D. disillusionment with *management-by-objectives* on the part of a majority of managers

   4.____

5. Of the following, which is usually considered to be a MAJOR obstacle to the systematic analysis of potential problems by managers?
   A. Managers have a tendency to think that all the implications of some proposed step cannot be fully understood.
   B. Rewards rarely go to those managers who are most successful at resolving current problems in management.
   C. There is a common conviction of manages that their goals are difficult to achieve.
   D. Managers are far more concerned about correcting today's problems than with preventing tomorrow's.

   5.____

6. Which of the following should generally have the MOST influence on the selection of supervisors?
   A. Experience within the work unit where the vacancies exist
   B. Amount of money needed to effect the promotion
   C. Personal preferences of the administration
   D. Evaluation of capacity to exercise supervisory responsibilities

7. In questioning a potential administrator for selection purposes, the one of the following practices which is MOST desirable is to
   A. encourage the job applicant to give primarily *yes* or *no* replies
   B. get the applicant to talk freely and in detail about his background
   C. let the job applicant speak most of the time
   D. probe the applicant's attitudes, motivation, and willingness to accept responsibility

8. In implementing the managerial function of training subordinates, it is USEFUL to know that a widely agreed-upon definition of human learning is that learning
   A. is a relatively permanent change in behavior that results from reinforced practice or experience
   B. involves an improvement, but not necessarily a change in behavior
   C. involves a change in behavior, but not necessarily an improvement
   D. is a temporary change in behavior which must be subject to practice or experience

9. If a manager were thinking about using a committee of subordinates to solve an operating problem, which of the following would generally NOT be an advantage of such use of the committee approach?
   A. Improved coordination   B. Low cost
   C. Increased motivation   D. Integrated judgment

10. Which one of the following management approaches MOST often uses model-building techniques to solve management problems?
    _____ approach.
    A. Behavioral   B. Fiscal   C. Quantitative   D. Process

11. Of the following, the MOST serious risk in using budgets as a tool for management control is the
    A. probable neglect of other good management practices
    B. likelihood of guesswork because of the need to plan far in advance
    C. possibility of undue emphasis on factors that are easiest to measure
    D. danger of making qualitative rather than quantitative assessments of performance

12. In government budgeting, the problem of relating financial transactions to the fiscal year in which they are budgeted is BEST met by
    A. determining the cash balance by comparing how much money has been received and how much has been paid out
    B. applying net revenue to the fiscal year in which they are collected as offset by relevant expenses

C. adopting a system whereby appropriations are entered when they are received and expenditures are entered when they are paid out
D. entering expenditures on the books when the obligation to make the expenditure is made

13. If the agency's bookkeeping system records income when it is received and expenditures when the money is paid out this system is USUALLY known as a _____ system.
    A. cash
    B. flow-payment
    C. deferred
    D. fiscal year income

14. An audit, as the term applies to budget execution, is MOST NEARLY a
    A. procedure based on the budget estimates
    B. control exercised by the executive on the legislature in the establishment of program priorities
    C. check on the legality of expenditures and is based on the appropriations act
    D. requirement which must be met before funds can be spent

15. In government budgeting, there is a procedure known as *allotment.*
    Of the following statements which relate to allotment, select the one that is MOST generally considered to be correct.
    Allotment
    A. increases the practice of budget units coming back to the legislature branch for supplemental appropriations
    B. is simply an example of red tape
    C. eliminates the requirement of timing of expenditures
    D. is designed to prevent waste

16. In government budgeting, the establishment of the schedules of allotments is MOST generally the responsibility of the
    A. budget unit and the legislature
    B. budget unit and the executive
    C. budget unit only
    D. executive and the legislature

17. Of the following statements relating to preparation of an organization's budget request, which is the MOST generally valid precaution?
    A. Give specific instructions on the format or budget requests and required supporting data
    B. Because of the complexity of preparing a budget request, avoid argumentation to support the requests
    C. Put requests in whatever format is desirable
    D. Consider that final approval will be given to initial estimates

18. Of the following statements which relate to the budget process in a well-organized government, select the one that is MOST NEARLY correct.
    A. The budget cycle is the step-by-step process which is repeated each and every fiscal year.
    B. Securing approval of the budget does not take place within the budget cycle.

4 (#2)

C. The development of a new budget and putting it into effect is a two-step process known as the budget cycle.
D. The fiscal period, usually a fiscal year, has no relation to the budget cycle.

19. If a manager were asked what PPBS stands for, he would be RIGHT if he said _____ budgeting system.
    A. public planning
    B. planning programming
    C. planning projections
    D. programming procedures

19._____

Questions 20-21.

DIRECTIONS: Questions 20 and 21 are to be answered on the basis of the following information.

Sample Budget

Refuse Collection	Amount
Personal Services	$30,000
Contractual Services	5,000
Supplies and Materials	5,000
Capital Outlay	10,000
	$50,000

Residential Collections	
Dwellings – 1 pickup per week	1,000
Tons of refuse collected per year	375
Cost of collections per ton	$ 8
Cost per dwelling pickup per year	$ 3
Total annual cost	$3,000

20. The sample budget shown is a simplified example of a _____ budget.
    A. factorial   B. performance   C. qualitative   D. rational

20._____

21. The budget shown in the sample differs CHIEFLY from line-item and program budgets in that it includes
    A. objects of expenditure but not activities or functions
    B. only activities, functions, and control
    C. activities and functions but not objects of expenditures
    D. levels of service

21._____

Question 22.

DIRECTIONS: Question 22 is to be answered on the basis of the following information.

5 (#2)

Sample Budget

Environmental Safety
  Air Pollution Protection
    Personal Services $20,000,000
    Contractual Services   4,000,000
    Supplies and Materials   4,000,000
    Capital Outlay   2,000,000
      Total Air Pollution Protection $30,000,000

  Water Pollution Protection
    Personal Services $23,000,000
    Supplies and Materials   4,500,000
    Capital Outlay   20,500,000
      Total Water Pollution Protection $48,000,000

Total Environmental Safety $78,000,000

22. Based on the above budget, which is the MOST valid statement?   22.____
    A. Environmental Safety, Air Pollution Protection, and Water Pollution Protection could all be considered program elements.
    B. The object listings included water pollution protection and capital outlay.
    C. Examples of the program element listings in the above are personal services and supplies and materials
    D. Contractual Services and Environmental Safety were the program element listings.

23. Which of the following is NOT an advantage of a program budget over a line-item budget?   23.____
A program budget
    A. allows us to set up priority lists in deciding what activities we will spend our money on
    B. gives us more control over expenditures than a line-item budget
    C. is more informative in that we know the broad purposes of spending money
    D. enables us to see if one program is getting much less money than the others

24. If a manager were trying to explain the fundamental difference between traditional accounting theory and practice and the newer practice of managerial accounting, he would be MOST accurate if he said that   24.____
    A. traditional accounting practice focused on providing information for persons outside organizations, while managerial accounting focuses on providing information for people inside organizations
    B. traditional accounting practice focused on providing information for persons inside organizations while managerial accounting focuses on providing information for persons outside organizations

C. managerial accounting is exclusively concerned with historical facts while traditional accounting stresses future projections exclusively
D. traditional accounting practice is more budget-focused than managerial accounting

25. Which of the following formulas is used to determine the number of days required to process work? 25.____
_____ = Days to Process Work

A. $\dfrac{\text{Employees x Daily Output}}{\text{Volume}}$

B. $\dfrac{\text{Volume x Daily Output}}{\text{Volume}}$

C. $\dfrac{\text{Volume}}{\text{Employees x Daily Output}}$

D. $\dfrac{\text{Employees x Volume}}{\text{Daily Output}}$

KEY (CORRECT ANSWERS)

1.	C		11.	C
2.	C		12.	D
3.	D		13.	A
4.	B		14.	C
5.	D		15.	D
6.	D		16.	C
7.	D		17.	A
8.	A		18.	A
9.	B		19.	B
10.	C		20.	B

21. D
22. A
23. B
24. A
25. C

TEST 3

DIRECTIONS: Each question or incomplete statement is followed by several suggested answers or completions. Select the one that BEST answers the question or completes the statement. *PRINT THE LETTER OF THE CORRECT ANSWER IN THE SPACE AT THE RIGHT.*

1. Electronic data processing equipment can produce more information faster than can be generated by any other means.
   In view of this, the MOST important problem faced by management at present is to
   A. keep computers fully occupied
   B. find enough computer personnel
   C. assimilate and properly evaluate the information
   D. obtain funds to establish appropriate information systems

   1.____

2. A well-designed management information system ESSENTIALLY provides each executive and manager the information he needs for
   A. determining computer time requirements
   B. planning and measuring results
   C. drawing a new organization chart
   D. developing a new office layout

   2.____

3. It is generally agreed that management policies should be periodically reappraised and restated in accordance with current conditions.
   Of the following, the approach which would be MOST effective in determining whether a policy should be revised is to
   A. conduct interviews with staff members at all levels in order to ascertain the relationship between the policy and actual practice
   B. make proposed revisions in the policy and apply it to current problems
   C. make up hypothetical situations using both the old policy and a revised version in order to make comparisons
   D. call a meeting of top level staff in order to discuss ways of revising the policy

   3.____

4. Every manager has many occasions to lead a conference or participate in a conference of some sort.
   Of the following statements that pertain to conferences and conference leadership, which is generally considered to be MOST valid?
   A. Since World War II, the trend has been toward fewer shared decisions and more conferences.
   B. The most important part of a conference leader's job is to direct discussion.
   C. In providing opportunities for group interaction, management should avoid consideration of its past management philosophy.
   D. A good administrator cannot lead a good conference if he is a poor public speaker.

   4.____

2 (#3)

5. Of the following, it is usually LEAST desirable for a conference leader to
   A. turn the question to the person who asked it
   B. summarize proceedings periodically
   C. make a practice of not repeating questions
   D. ask a question without indicating who is to reply

6. The behavioral school of management thought bases its beliefs on certain assumptions.
   Which of the following is NOT a belief of this school of thought?
   A. People tend to seek and accept responsibility.
   B. Most people can be creative in solving problems.
   C. People prefer security above all else.
   D. Commitment is the most important factor in motivating people.

7. The one of the following objectives which would be LEAST appropriate as a major goal of research in the field of human resources management is to
   A. predict future conditions, events, and manpower needs
   B. evaluate established policies, programs, and practices
   C. evaluate proposed policies, programs, and practices
   D. identify deficient organizational units and apply suitable penalties

8. Of the following general interviewing methods or techniques, the one that is USUALLY considered to be effective in counseling, grievances, and appraisal interviews is the _____ interview.
   A. directed   B. non-directed   C. panel   D. patterned

9. The ESSENTIAL first phase of decision-making is
   A. finding alternative solutions
   B. making a diagnosis of the problem
   C. selecting the plan to follow
   D. analyzing and comparing alternative solutions

10. Assume that, in a certain organization, a situation has developed in which there is little difference in status or authority between individuals.
    Which of the following would be the MOST likely result with regard to communication in this organization?
    A. Both the accuracy and flow of communication will be improved.
    B. Both the accuracy and flow of communication will substantially decrease.
    C. Employees will seek more formal lines of communication.
    D. Neither the flow nor the accuracy of communication will be improved over the former hierarchical structure.

11. The main function of many agency administrative offices is *information management*. Information that is received by an administrative officer may be classified as active or passive, depending upon whether or not it requires the recipient to take some action.

Of the following, the item received which is clearly the MOST active information is
- A. an appointment of a new staff member
- B. a payment voucher for a new desk
- C. a press release concerning a past city event
- D. the minutes of a staff meeting

12. Which one of the following sets BEST describes the general order in which to teach an operation to a new employee?
    - A. Prepare, present, tryout, follow-up
    - B. Prepare, test, tryout, re-test
    - C. Present, test, tryout, follow-up
    - D. Test, present, follow-up, re-test

13. Of the following, public employees may be separated from public service
    - A. for the same reasons which are generally acceptable for discharging employees in private industry
    - B. only under the most trying circumstances
    - C. under procedures that are neither formalized nor subject to review
    - D. solely in extreme cases involving offenses of gravest character

14. Of the following, the one LEAST considered to be a communication barrier is
    - A. group feedback
    - B. charged words
    - C. selective perception
    - D. symbolic meanings

15. Of the following ways for a manager to handle his appointments, the BEST way, according to experts in administration, generally is to
    - A. schedule his own appointments and inform his secretary not to reserve his time without his approval
    - B. encourage everyone to make appointments through his secretary and tell her when he makes his own appointments
    - C. see no one who has not made a previous appointment
    - D. permit anyone to see him without an appointment

16. Assume that a manager decides to examine closely one of five units under his supervision to uncover problems common to all five.
    His research technique is MOST closely related to the method called
    - A. experimentation
    - B. simulation
    - C. linear analysis
    - D. sampling

17. If one views the process of management as a dynamic process, which one of the following functions is NOT a legitimate part of that process?
    - A. Communication
    - B. Decision-making
    - C. Organizational slack
    - D. Motivation

18. Which of the following would be the BEST statement of a budget-oriented purpose for a government administrator? To
    A. provide 200 hours of instruction in basic reading for 3,500 adult illiterates at a cost of $1 million in the next fiscal year
    B. inform the public of adult educational programs
    C. facilitate the transfer to a city agency of certain functions of a federally-funded program which is being phased out
    D. improve the reading skills of the adult citizens in the city

19. Modern management philosophy and practices are changing to accommodate the expectations and motivations of organization personnel.
    Which of the following terms INCORRECTLY describes these newer managerial approaches?
    A. Rational management
    B. Participative management
    C. Decentralization
    D. Democratic supervision

20. Management studies support the hypothesis that, in spite of the tendency of employees to censor the information communicated to their supervisor, subordinates are MORE likely to communicate problem-oriented information upward when they have
    A. a long period of service in the organization
    B. a high degree of trust in the supervisor
    C. a high educational level
    D. low status on the organizational ladder

KEY (CORRECT ANSWERS)

1.	C	11.	A
2.	B	12.	A
3.	A	13.	A
4.	B	14.	A
5.	A	15.	B
6.	C	16.	D
7.	D	17.	C
8.	B	18.	A
9.	B	19.	A
10.	D	20.	B

EXAMINATION SECTION
TEST 1

DIRECTIONS: Each question or incomplete statement is followed by several suggested answers or completions. Select the one that BEST answers the question or completes the statement. *PRINT THE LETTER OF THE CORRECT ANSWER IN THE SPACE AT THE RIGHT.*

1. At times there may be a conflict between employees' needs and agency goals. A supervisor's MAIN role in motivating employees in such circumstances is to try to
    A. develop good work habits among the employees whom he supervises
    B. emphasize the importance of material rewards such as merit increases
    C. keep careful records of employees' performance for possible disciplinary action
    D. reconcile employees' objectives with those of the public agency

1.____

2. Organizations cannot function effectively without policies.
However, when an organization imposes excessively detailed policy restrictions, it is MOST likely to lead to
    A. conflicts among individual employees
    B. a lack of adequate supervision
    C. a reduction of employee initiative
    D. a reliance on punitive discipline

2.____

3. The PRIMARY responsibility for establishing good employee relations in the public service usually rests with
    A. employees
    B. management
    C. civil service organizations
    D. employee organizations

3.____

4. At times, certain off-the-job conduct of public employees may be of concern to management. This concern stems from the fact that
    A. agency programs could be harmed by adverse publicity if employees' conduct is considered detrimental by the public
    B. fairness to all concerned is usually the major consideration in disciplinary cases
    C. public employees must meet higher standards than employees working in private industry
    D. public employees have high ethical standards and may participate in social action programs

4.____

5. At one time or another, most employees ask for, or expect, special treatment. For a supervisor faced with this problem, the one of the following which is the MOST valid guideline is:
    A. According to the rules, a supervisor must give identical treatment to all his subordinates, regardless of the circumstances.

5.____

B. Although all employees have equal rights, it is sometimes necessary to give an employee special treatment to meet an individual need.
C. It would damage morale if any employee were to receive special treatment, regardless of circumstances.
D. Since each employee has different needs, there is little reason to maintain general rules.

6. Mental health problems exist in many parts of our society and may also be found in the work setting.
   The BASIC role of the supervisor in relation to the mental health problems of his subordinates is to
   A. restrict himself solely to the taking of disciplinary measures, if warranted, and follow up carefully
   B. avoid involvement in personal matters
   C. identify mental health problems as early as possible
   D. resolve mental health problems through personal counseling

7. Supervisory expectation of high levels of employee performance, where such performance is possible, is MOST likely to lead to employees'
   A. expecting frequent praise and encouragement
   B. gaining a greater sense of satisfaction
   C. needing less detailed instructions than previously
   D. reducing their quantitative output

8. In public agencies, as elsewhere, supervisors sometimes compete with one another to increase their units' productivity.
   Of the following, the MAJOR disadvantage of such competition, from the general viewpoint of providing good public service, is that
   A. while individual employee effort will increase, unit productivity will decrease
   B. employees will be discouraged from sincere interest in their work
   C. the supervisors' competition may hinder the achievement of agency goals
   D. total payroll costs will increase as the activities of each unit increase

9. If employees are motivated primarily by material compensation, the amount of effort an individual employee will put into performing his work effectively will depend MAINLY upon how he perceives
   A. cooperation to be tied to successful effort
   B. the association between good work and increased compensation
   C. the public status of his particular position
   D. the supervisor's behavior in work situations

10. Cash awards to individual employees are sometimes used to encourage useful suggestions. However, some management experts believe that awards should involve some form of employee recognition other than cash.
    Which of the following reasons BEST supports opposition to using cash as a reward for worthwhile suggestions?

A. Cash awards cause employees to expend excessive time in making suggestions.
B. Taxpayer opposition to dash awards has increased following generous salary increases for public employees in recent years.
C. Public funds expended on awards leads to a poor image of public employees.
D. The use of cash awards raises the problem of deciding the monetary value of suggestions.

11. The BEST general rule for a supervisor to follow in giving praise and criticism is to
    A. criticize and praise publicly
    B. criticize publicly and praise privately
    C. praise and criticize privately
    D. praise publicly and criticize privately

12. An important step in designing an error-control policy is to determine the maximum number of errors that can be considered acceptable for the entire organization.
    Of the following, the MOST important factor in making such a decision is the
    A. number of clerical staff available to check for errors
    B. frequency of errors by supervisors
    C. human and material costs of errors
    D. number of errors that will become known to the public

13. When a supervisor tries to correct a situation where errors have been widespread, he should concentrate his efforts, and those of the employees involved, on
    A. avoiding future mistakes
    B. fixing appropriate blame
    C. preparing a written report
    D. determining fair penalties

14. When delegating work to a subordinate, a supervisor should ALWAYS tell the subordinate
    A. each step in the procedure for doing the work
    B. how much time to expend
    C. what is to be accomplished
    D. whether reports are necessary

15. The responsibilities of all employees should be clearly defined and understood. In addition, in order for employees to successfully fulfill their responsibilities, they should also GENERALLY be given
    A. written directives
    B. close supervision
    C. corresponding authority
    D. daily instructions

16. The one of the following types of training in which positive transfer of training to the actual work situation is MOST likely to take place is _____ training.
    A. conference
    B. demonstration
    C. classroom
    D. on-the-job

17. The type of training or instruction in which the subject matter is presented in small units called frames is known as
    A. programmed instruction
    B. reinforcement
    C. remediation
    D. skills training

    17.____

18. In order to bring about maximum learning in a training situation, a supervisor acting as a trainer should attempt to create a setting in which
    A. all trainees experience a large amount of failure as an incentive
    B. all trainees experience a small amount of failure as an incentive
    C. each trainee experiences approximately the same amounts of success and failure
    D. each trainee experiences as much success and as little failure as possible

    18.____

19. Assume that, in a training course given by an agency, the instructor conducts a brief quiz, on paper, toward the close of each session.
    From the point of view of maximizing learning, it would be BEST for the instructor to
    A. wait until the last session to provide the correct answers
    B. give the correct answers aloud immediately after each quiz
    C. permit trainees to take the questions home with them so that they can look up the answers
    D. wait until the next session to provide the correct answers

    19.____

20. A supervisor, in the course of evaluating employees, should ALWAYS determine whether
    A. employees realize that their work is under scrutiny
    B. the ratings will be included in permanent records
    C. employees meet standards of performance
    D. his statements on the rating form are similar to those made by the previous supervisor

    20.____

21. All of the following are legitimate objectives of employee performance reporting systems EXCEPT
    A. serving as a check on personnel policies such as job qualification requirements and placement techniques
    B. determining who is the least efficient worker among a large number of employees
    C. improving employee performance by identifying strong and weak points in individual performance
    D. developing standards of satisfactory performance

    21.____

22. Studies of existing employee performance evaluation schemes have revealed a common tendency to construct guides in order to measure inferred traits.
    Of the following, the BEST example of an inferred trait is
    A. appearance   B. loyalty   C. accuracy   D. promptness

    22.____

5 (#1)

23. Which of the following is MOST likely to be a positive influence in promoting common agreement at a staff conference?
    A. A mature, tolerant group of participants
    B. A strong chairman with firm opinions
    C. The normal differences of human personalities
    D. The urge to forcefully support one's views

    23.____

24. Before holding a problem-solving conference, the conference leader sent to each invitee an announcement on which he listed the names of all invitees. His action in listing the names was
    A. *wise*, mainly because all invitees will know who has been invited, and can, if necessary, plan a proper approach
    B. *unwise*, mainly because certain invitees could form factions prior to the conference
    C. *unwise*, mainly because invitees might come to the conference in a belligerent mood if they had had interpersonal conflicts with other invitees
    D. *wise*, mainly because invitees who are antagonistic to each other could decide not to attend

    24.____

25. Methods analysis is a detailed study of existing or proposed work methods for the purpose of improving agency operations.
    Of the following, it is MOST accurate to say that this type of study
    A. can sometimes be made informally by the experienced supervisor who can identify problems and suggest solutions
    B. is not suitable for studying the operations of a public agency
    C. will be successfully accomplished only if an outside organization reviews agency operations
    D. usually costs more to complete than is justified by the potential economies to be realized

    25.____

KEY (CORRECT ANSWERS)

1.	D	11.	D
2.	C	12.	C
3.	B	13.	A
4.	A	14.	C
5.	B	15.	C
6.	C	16.	D
7.	B	17.	A
8.	C	18.	D
9.	B	19.	B
10.	D	20.	C

21.
22. B
23. A
24. A
25. A

TEST 2

DIRECTIONS: Each question or incomplete statement is followed by several suggested answers or completions. Select the one that BEST answers the question or completes the statement. *PRINT THE LETTER OF THE CORRECT ANSWER IN THE SPACE AT THE RIGHT.*

1. Present-day managerial practices advocate that adequate hierarchical levels of communication be maintained among all levels of management.
   Of the following, the BEST way to accomplish this is with
   A. intradepartmental memoranda only
   B. interdepartmental memoranda only
   C. periodic staff meetings, interdepartmental and intradepartmental memoranda
   D. interdepartmental and intradepartmental memoranda

   1.____

2. It is generally agreed upon that it is important to have effective communications in the unit so that everyone knows exactly what is expected of him.
   Of the following, the communications system which can assist in fulfilling this objective BEST is one which consists of
   A. written policies and procedures for administrative functions and verbal policies and procedures for professional functions
   B. written policies and procedures for professional and administrative functions
   C. verbal policies and procedures for professional and administrative functions
   D. verbal policies and procedures for professional functions

   2.____

3. If a department manager wishes to build an effective department, he MOST generally must
   A. be able to hire and fire as he feels necessary
   B. consider the total aspects of his job, his influence and the effects of his decisions
   C. have access to reasonable amounts of personnel and money with which to build his programs
   D. attend as many professional conferences as possible so that he can keep up-to-date with all the latest advances in the field

   3.____

4. Of the following, the factor which generally contributes MOST effectively to the performance of the unit is that the supervisor
   A. personally inspect the work of all employees
   B. fill orders at a faster rate than his subordinates
   C. have an exact knowledge of theory
   D. implement a program of professional development for his staff

   4.____

5. Administrative policies relate MOST closely to
   A. control of commodities and personnel
   B. general policies emanating from the central office
   C. fiscal management of the department only
   D. handling and dispensing of funds

   5.____

2 (#2)

6. Part of being a good supervisor is to be able to develop an attitude towards employees which will motivate them to do their best on the job.
The GOOD supervisor, therefore, should
   A. take an interest in subordinates, but not develop an all-consuming attitude in this area
   B. remain in an aloof position when dealing with employees
   C. be as close to subordinates as possible on the job
   D. take a complete interest in all the activities of subordinates, both on and off the job

6.____

7. The practice of a supervisor assigning an experienced employee to train new employees instead of training them himself is GENERALLY considered
   A. *undesirable*; the more experienced employee will resent being taken away from his regular job
   B. *desirable*; the supervisor can then devote more time to his regular duties
   C. *undesirable*; the more experienced employee is not working at the proper level to train new employees
   D. *desirable*; the more experienced employee is probably a better trainer than the supervisor

7.____

8. It is generally agreed that on-the-job training is MOST effective when new employees are
   A. provided with study manuals, standard operating procedures and other written materials to be studied for at least two weeks before the employees attempt to do the job
   B. shown how to do the job in detail, and then instructed to do the work under close supervision
   C. trained by an experienced worker for at least a week to make certain that the employees can do the job
   D. given work immediately which is checked at the end of each day

8.____

9. Employees sometimes form small informal groups, commonly called cliques. With regard to the effect of such groups on processing of the workload, the attitude a supervisor should take towards these cliques is that of
   A. *acceptance*, since they take the employees' minds off their work without wasting too much time
   B. *rejection*, since those workers inside the clique tend to do less work than the outsiders
   C. *acceptance*, since the supervisor is usually included in the clique
   D. *rejection*, since they are usually disliked by higher management

9.____

10. Of the following, the BEST statement regarding rules and regulations in a unit is that they
    A. are "necessary evils" to be tolerated by those at and above the first supervisory level only
    B. are stated in broad, indefinite terms so as to allow maximum amount of leeway in complying with them

10.____

C. must be understood by all employees in the unit
D. are primarily for management's needs since insurance regulations mandate them

11. It is sometimes considered desirable for a supervisor to survey the opinions of his employees before taking action on decisions affecting them.
Of the following the greatest DISADVANTAGE of following this approach is that the employees might
    A. use this opportunity to complain rather than to make constructive suggestions
    B. lose respect for their supervisor whom they feel cannot make his own decisions
    C. regard this as an attempt by the supervisor to get ideas for which he can later claim credit
    D. be resentful if their suggestions are not adopted

12. Of the following, the MOST important reason for keeping statements of duties of employees up-to-date is to
    A. serve as a basis of information for other governmental jurisdictions
    B. enable the department of personnel to develop job-related examinations
    C. differentiate between levels within the occupational groups
    D. enable each employee to know what his duties are

13. Of the following, the BEST way to evaluate the progress of a new subordinate is to
    A. compare the output of the new employee from week to week as to quantity and quality
    B. obtain the opinions of the new employee's co-workers
    C. test the new employee periodically to see how much he has learned
    D. hold frequent discussions with the employee focusing on his work

14. Of the following, a supervisor is LEAST likely to contribute to good morale in the unit if he
    A. encourages employees to increase their knowledge and proficiency in their work on their own time
    B. reprimands subordinates uniformly when infractions are committed
    C. refuses to accept explanations for mistakes regardless of who has made them or how serious they are
    D. compliments subordinates for superior work performance in the presence of their peers

15. The practice of promoting supervisors from within a given unit only, rather than from within the entire agency, may BEST be described as
    A. *desirable*, because the type of work in each unit generally is substantially different from all other units
    B. *undesirable*, since it will severely reduce the number of eligible from which to select a supervisor

C. *desirable*, since it enables each employee to know in advance the precise extent of promotion opportunities in his unit
D. *undesirable*, because it creates numerous administrative and budgetary difficulties

16. Of the following, the BEST way for a supervisor to make assignments GENERALLY is to
    A. give the easier assignments to employees with greater seniority
    B. give the difficult assignments to the employees with greater seniority
    C. make assignments according to the ability of each employee
    D. rotate the assignments among the employees

17. Assume that a supervisor makes a proposal through appropriate channels which would delegate final authority and responsibility to a subordinate employee for a major control function within the agency.
    According to current management theory, this proposal should be
    A. *adopted*, since this would enable the supervisor to devote more time to non-routine tasks
    B. *rejected*, since final responsibility for this high-level assignment may not properly be delegated to a subordinate employee
    C. *adopted*, since the assignment of increased responsibility to subordinate employees is a vital part of their development and training
    D. *rejected*, since the morale of the subordinate employees not selected for this assignment would be adversely affected

18. If it becomes necessary for a supervisor to improve the performance of a subordinate to assure the achievement of results according to plans, the BEST course of action, of the following, generally would be to
    A. emphasize the subordinate's strengths and try to motivate the employee to improve on those factors
    B. emphasize the subordinate's weak areas of performance and try to bring them up to an acceptable standard
    C. issue a memorandum to all employees warning that if performance does not improve, disciplinary measures will be taken
    D. transfer the subordinate to another section engaged in different work

19. A supervisor who specifies each phase of a job in detail supervises closely and permits very little discretion in performance of tasks GENERALLY
    A. provides motivation for his staff to produce more work
    B. finds that his subordinate make fewer mistakes than those with minimal supervision
    C. finds that his subordinates have little or no incentive to work any harder than necessary
    D. provides superior training opportunities for his employees

20. Assume that you supervise two employees who do not get along well with each other. Their relationship has been continuously deteriorating. You decide to take steps to solve this problem by first determining the reason for their inability to get along with each other.
    This course of action is
    A. *desirable*, because their work is probably adversely affected by their differences
    B. *undesirable*, because your inquiries might be misinterpreted by the employees and cause resentment
    C. *desirable*, because you could then learn who is at fault for causing the deteriorating relationship and take appropriate disciplinary measures
    D. *undesirable*, because it is best to let them work their differences out between themselves

21. Routine procedures that have worked well in the past should be reviewed periodically by a supervisor MAINLY because
    A. they may have become outdated or in need of revision
    B. employees may dislike the procedures even though they have proven successful in the past
    C. these reviews are the main part of a supervisor's job
    D. this practice serves to give the supervisor an idea of how productive his subordinates are

22. Assume that an employee tells his supervisor about a grievance he has against a co-worker. The supervisor assures the employee that he will immediately take action to eliminate the grievance.
    The supervisor's attitude should be considered
    A. *correct*, because a good supervisor is one who can come to a quick decision
    B. *incorrect*, because the supervisor should have told the employee that he will investigate the grievance and then determine a future course of action
    C. *correct*, because the employee's morale will be higher, resulting in greater productivity
    D. *incorrect*, because the supervisor should remain uninvolved and let the employees settle grievances between themselves

23. If an employee's work output is low and of poor quality due to faulty work habits, the MOST constructive of the following ways for a supervisor to correct this situation *generally* is to
    A. discipline the employee
    B. transfer the employee to another unit
    C. provide additional training
    D. check the employee's work continuously

24. Assume that it becomes necessary for a supervisor to ask his staff to work overtime.
    Which one of the following techniques is MOST likely to win their willing cooperation to do this?

A. Point out that this is part of their job specification entitled "performs related work"
B. Explain the reason it is necessary for the employees to work overtime
C. Promise the employees special consideration regarding future leave matters
D. Warn that if the employees do not work overtime, they will face possible disciplinary action

25. If an employee's work performance has recently fallen below established minimum standards for quality and quantity, the threat of demotion or other disciplinary measures as an attempt to improve this employee's performance would probably be the MOST acceptable and effective course of action
    A. *only* after other more constructive measures have failed
    B. *if* applied uniformly to all employees as soon as performance falls below standard
    C. *only* if the employee understands that the threat will not actually be carried out
    D. *if* the employee is promised that, as soon as his work performance improves, he will be reinstated to his previous status

25.____

KEY (CORRECT ANSWERS)

1.	C		11.	D
2.	B		12.	D
3.	B		13.	A
4.	D		14.	C
5.	A		15.	B
6.	A		16.	C
7.	B		17.	B
8.	B		18.	B
9.	A		19.	C
10.	C		20.	A

21. A
22. B
23. C
24. B
25. A

TEST 3

DIRECTIONS: Each question or incomplete statement is followed by several suggested answers or completions. Select the one that BEST answers the question or completes the statement. *PRINT THE LETTER OF THE CORRECT ANSWER IN THE SPACE AT THE RIGHT.*

1. If, as a supervisor, it becomes necessary for you to assign an employee to supervise your unit during your vacation, it would generally be BEST to select the employee who
    A. is the best technician on the staff
    B. can get the work out smoothly, without friction
    C. has the most seniority
    D. is the most popular with the group

    1.____

2. Assume that, as a supervisor, your own work has accumulated to the point where you decide that it is desirable for you to delegate in order to meet your deadlines.
    The one of the following tasks which would be MOST appropriate to delegate to a subordinate is
    A. checking the work of the employees for accuracy
    B. attending a staff conference at which implementation of a new departmental policy will be discussed
    C. preparing a final report including a recommendation on purchase of expensive new laboratory equipment
    D. preparing final budget estimates for next year's budget

    2.____

3. Of the following actions, the one LEAST appropriate for you to take during an initial interview with a new employee is to
    A. find out about the experience and education of the new employee
    B. attempt to determine for what job in your unit the employee would best be suited
    C. tell the employee about his duties and responsibilities
    D. ascertain whether the employee will make good promotion material

    3.____

4. If it becomes necessary to reprimand a subordinate employee, the BEST of the following ways to do this is to
    A. ask the employee to stay after working hours and then reprimand him
    B. reprimand the employee immediately after the infraction has been committed
    C. take the employee aside and speak to him privately during regular working hours
    D. write a short memo to the employee warning that strict adherence to departmental policy and procedures is required of all employees

    4.____

5. If you, as a supervisor, believe that one of your subordinate employees has a serious problem, such as alcoholism or an emotional disturbance, which is adversely affecting his work, the BEST way to handle this situation *initially* would be to

    5.____

A. urge him to seek proper professional help before he is dismissed from his job
B. ignore it and let the employee work out the problem himself
C. suggest that the employee take an extended leave of absence until he can again function effectively
D. frankly tell the employee that unless his work improves, you will take disciplinary measures against him

6. Of the following, the BEST way to develop a subordinate's potential is to
   A. give him a fair chance to learn by doing
   B. assign him more than his share of work
   C. criticize only his work
   D. urge him to do his work rapidly

6._____

7. During a survey, an employee from another agency asks you to assist him on a job which would require a full day of your time.
   Of the following, the BEST immediate action for you to take is to
   A. refuse to assist him
   B. ask for compensation before doing it
   C. assist him promptly
   D. notify his department head

7._____

8. Of the following, the BEST way to handle an overly talkative subordinate is to
   A. have your superior talk to him about it
   B. have a subordinate talk to him about it
   C. talk to him about it in a group conference
   D. talk to him about it in private

8._____

9. While you are making a survey, a citizen questions you about the work you are doing.
   Of the following, the BEST thing to do is to
   A. answer the questions tactfully
   B. refuse to answer any questions
   C. advise him to write a letter to the main office
   D. answer the questions in double-talk

9._____

10. Respect for a supervisor is MOST likely to increase if he is
    A. morose   B. sporadic   C. vindictive   D. zealous

10._____

11. A subordinate who continuously bypasses his immediate supervisor for technical information should be
    A. reprimanded by his immediate supervisor
    B. ignored by his immediate supervisor
    C. given more difficult work to do
    D. given less difficult work to do

11._____

12. Complicated instructions should NOT be written
    A. accurately   B. lucidly   C. factually   D. verbosely

12._____

13. Of the following, the MOST important reason for checking a report is to
    A. check accuracy
    B. eliminate unnecessary sections
    C. catch mistakes
    D. check for delineation

14. Two subordinates under your supervision dislike each other to the extent that production is cut down.
    Your BEST action as a supervisor is to
    A. ignore the matter and hope for the best
    B. transfer the more aggressive man
    C. cut down on the workload
    D. talk to them together about the matter

15. One of the following characteristics which a supervisor should NOT display while explaining a job to a subordinate is
    A. enthusiasm   B. confidence   C. apathy   D. determination

16. Of the following, for BEST production of work, it should be assigned according to a person's
    A. attitude toward the work
    B. ability to do the work
    C. salary
    D. seniority

17. You receive an anonymous written complaint from a citizen about a subordinate who used abusive language.
    Of the following, your BEST course of action is to
    A. ignore the letter
    B. report it to your supervisor
    C. discuss the complaint with the subordinate privately
    D. keep the subordinate in the office

18. A supervisor should recognize that the way to get the BEST results from his instructions and assignments to the staff is to use
    A. a suggestive approach after he has decided exactly what is to be done and how
    B. the willing and cooperative staff members and avoid the hard-to-handle people
    C. care to select the persons most capable of carrying out the assignments
    D. an authoritative, non-nonsense tone when issuing instructions or giving assignments

19. As the supervisor of a unit, you find that you are spending too much of your time on routine tasks and not enough on coordinating the work of the staff or preparing necessary reports.
    Of the following, it would be MOST advisable for you to
    A. discard a great portion of the routine jobs done in the unit
    B. give some of the routine jobs to other members of the staff
    C. postpone the routine jobs and concentrate on coordinating the work of the staff
    D. delegate the job of coordinating the work to the most capable member of the staff

20. At times a supervisor may be called upon to train new employees. Suppose that you are giving such training in several sessions to be held on different days. During the first session, a trainee interrupts several times to ask questions at key points in your discussion.
    Of the following, the BEST way to handle this trainee is to
    A. advise him to pay closer attention so he can avoid asking too many questions
    B. tell him to listen without interrupting and he'll hear his questions answered
    C. answer his questions to show him that you know your field, but make a mental note that this trainee is a troublemaker
    D. answer each question fully and make certain he understands the answers

21. Employee errors can be reduced to a minimum by effective supervision and by training.
    Which of the following approaches used by a supervisor would usually be MOST effective in handling an employee who has made an avoidable and serious error for the first time?
    A. Tell the worker how other employees avoid making errors
    B. Analyze with the employee the situation leading to the error and then take whatever administrative or training steps are needed to avoid such errors
    C. Use this error as the basis for a staff meeting at which the employee's error is disclosed and discussed in an effort to improve the performance
    D. Urge the employee to modify his behavior in light of his mistake

22. Suppose that a particular staff member, formerly one of your most regular workers, has recently fallen into the habit of arriving a bit late to work several times a week. You feel that such a habit can grow consistently worse and spread to other staff members unless it is checked.
    Of the following, the BEST action for you to take, as the supervisor in charge of the unit, is to
    A. go immediately to your own supervisor, present the facts, and have this employee disciplined
    B. speak privately to this tardy employee, advise him of the need to improve his punctuality, and inform him that he'll be disciplined if late again
    C. talk to the co-worker with whom this late employee is most friendly, and ask the friend to help him solve his tardiness problem
    D. speak privately with this employee, and try to discover and deal with the reasons for the latenesses

23. A supervisor may make an assignment in the form of a request, a command, or a call for volunteers.
    It is LEAST desirable to make an assignment in the form of a request when
    A. an employee does not like the particular kind of assignment to be given
    B. the assignment requires working past the regular closing day
    C. an emergency has come up
    D. the assignment is not particularly pleasant for anybody

24. When you give a certain task that you normally perform yourself to one of your employees, it is MOST important that you
    A. lead the employee to believe that he has been chosen above others to perform this job
    B. describe the job as important even though it is merely a routine task
    C. explain the job that needs to be accomplished, but always let the employee decide how to do it
    D. tell the employee why you are delegating the job to him and explain exactly what he is to do

25. A supervisor when instructing new trainees in the routine of his unit should include a description of the department's overall objectives and programs in order to
    A. insure that individual work assignments will be completed satisfactorily
    B. create a favorable impression of his supervisory capabilities
    C. develop a better understanding of the purposes behind work assignments
    D. produce an immediate feeling of group cooperation

KEY (CORRECT ANSWERS)

1.	B		11.	A
2.	A		12.	D
3.	D		13.	C
4.	C		14.	D
5.	A		15.	C
6.	A		16.	B
7.	A		17.	C
8.	D		18.	C
9.	A		19.	B
10.	D		20.	D

21.	B
22.	D
23.	A
24.	D
25.	C

TEST 4

DIRECTIONS: Each question or incomplete statement is followed by several suggested answers or completions. Select the one that BEST answers the question or completes the statement. *PRINT THE LETTER OF THE CORRECT ANSWER IN THE SPACE AT THE RIGHT.*

1. An integral part of every supervisor's job is getting his ideas or instructions across to his staff.
   The extent of his success, if he has a reasonably competent staff, is PRIMARILY dependent on the
   A. interest of the employee
   B. intelligence of the employee
   C. reasoning behind the ideas or instructions
   D. presentation of the ideas or instructions

   1.____

2. Generally, what is the FIRST action the supervisor should take when an employee approaches him with a complaint?
   A. Review the employee's recent performance with him
   B. Use the complaint as a basis to discuss improvement of procedures
   C. Find out from the employee the details of the complaint
   D. Advise the employee to take his complaint to the head of the department

   2.____

3. Of the following, which is NOT usually considered one of the purposes of counseling an employee after an evaluation of his performance?
   A. Explaining the performance standards used by the supervisor
   B. Discussing necessary discipline action to be taken
   C. Emphasizing the employee's strengths and weaknesses
   D. Planning better utilization of the employee's strengths

   3.____

4. Assume that a supervisor, when reviewing a decision reached by one of his subordinates, finds the decision incorrect.
   Under these circumstances, it would be MOST desirable for the supervisor to
   A. correct the decision and inform the subordinate of this at a staff meeting
   B. correct the decision and suggest a more detailed analysis in the future
   C. help the employee find the reason for the correct decision
   D. refrain from assigning this type of a problem to the employee

   4.____

5. An IMPORTANT characteristic of a good supervisor is his ability to
   A. be a stern disciplinarian
   B. put off the settling of grievances
   C. solve problems
   D. find fault in individuals

   5.____

6. A new supervisor will BEST obtain the respect of the men assigned to him if he
   A. makes decisions rapidly and sticks to the, regardless of whether they are right or wrong
   B. makes decisions rapidly and then changes them just as rapidly if the decisions are wrong
   C. does not make any decisions unless he is absolutely sure that they are right
   D. makes his decisions after considering carefully all available information

   6.____

7. A newly appointed worker is operating at a level of performance below that of the other employees.
   In this situation, a supervisor should FIRST
   A. lower the acceptable standard for the new man
   B. find out why the new man cannot do as well as the others
   C. advise the new worker he will be dropped from the payroll at the end of the probationary period
   D. assign another new worker to assist the first man

8. Assume that you have to instruct a new man on a specific departmental operation. The new man seems unsure of what you have said.
   Of the following, the BEST way for you to determine whether the man has understood you is to
   A. have the man explain the operation to you in his own words
   B. repeat your explanation to him slowly
   C. repeat your explanation to him, using simpler wording
   D. emphasize the important parts of the operation to him

9. A supervisor realizes that he has taken an instantaneous dislike to a new worker assigned to him.
   The BEST course of action for the supervisor to take in this case is to
   A. be especially observant of the new worker's actions
   B. request that the new worker be reassigned
   C. make a special effort to be fair to the new worker
   D. ask to be transferred himself

10. A supervisor gives detailed instructions to his men as to how a certain type of job is to be done.
    One ADVANTAGE of this practice is that this will
    A. result in a more flexible operation
    B. standardize operations
    C. encourage new men to learn
    D. encourage initiative to learn

11. Of the following the one that would MOST likely be the result of poor planning is:
    A. Omissions are discovered after the work is completed
    B. During the course of normal inspection, a meter is found to be inaccessible
    C. An inspector completes his assignments for that day ahead of schedule
    D. A problem arises during an inspection and prevents an inspector from completing his day's assignments

12. Of the following, the BEST way for a supervisor to maintain good employee morale is for the supervisor to
    A. avoid correcting the employee when he makes mistakes
    B. continually praise the employee's work even when it is of average quality
    C. show that he is willing to assist in solving the employee's problems
    D. accept the employee's excuses for failure even though the excuses are not valid

13. A supervisor takes time to explain to his men why a departmental order has been issued.
    This practice is
    A. *good*, mainly because without this explanation the men will not be able to carry out the order
    B. *bad*, mainly because time will be wasted for no useful purpose
    C. *good*, because understanding the reasons behind an order will lead to more effective carrying out of the order
    D. *bad*, because men will then question every order that they receive

13.____

14. Of the following, the MOST important responsibility of a supervisor in charge of a section is to
    A. establish close personal relationships with each of his subordinates in the section
    B. insure that each subordinate in the section knows the full range of his duties and responsibilities
    C. maintain friendly relations with his immediate supervisor
    D. protect his subordinate from criticism from any source

14.____

15. The BEST way to get a good work output from employees is to
    A. hold over them the threat of disciplinary action or removal
    B. maintain a steady, unrelenting pressure on them
    C. show them that you can do anything they can do faster and better
    D. win their respect and liking, so they want to work for you

15.____

KEY (CORRECT ANSWERS)

1.	A	6.	D	11.	A
2.	C	7.	B	12.	C
3.	A	8.	A	13.	C
4.	C	9.	C	14.	B
5.	C	10.	B	15.	D

PREPARING WRITTEN MATERIAL
EXAMINATION SECTION
TEST 1

DIRECTIONS: Each of the sentences in this test may be classified under one of the following four categories:
- A. *Incorrect* because of faulty grammar or sentence structure
- B. *Incorrect* because of faulty punctuation
- C. *Incorrect* because of faulty capitalization
- D. *Correct*

Examine each sentence carefully to determine under which of the above four options it is best classified. Then, in the space at the right, print the capital letter preceding the option which is the BEST of the four suggested above.

(Each incorrect sentence contains but one type of error. Consider a sentence to be correct if it contains none of the types of errors mentioned, even though there may be other correct ways of expressing the same thought.)

1. This fact, together with those brought out at the previous meeting, prove that the schedule is satisfactory to the employees.   1.____

2. Like many employees in scientific fields, the work of bookkeepers and accountants requires accuracy and neatness.   2.____

3. "What can I do for you," the secretary asked as she motioned to the visitor to take a seat.   3.____

4. Our representative, Mr. Charles will call on you next week to determine whether or not your claim has merit.   4.____

5. We expect you to return in the spring; please do not disappoint us.   5.____

6. Any supervisor, who disregards the just complaints of his subordinates, is remiss in the performance of his duty.   6.____

7. Because she took less than an hour for lunch is no reason for permitting her to leave before five o'clock.   7.____

8. "Miss Smith," said the supervisor, "Please arrange a meeting of the staff for two o'clock on Monday."   8.____

9. A private company's vacation and sick leave allowance usually differs considerably from a public agency.   9.____

10. Therefore, in order to increase the efficiency of operations in the department, a report on the recommended changes in procedures was presented to the departmental committee in charge of the program.   10.____

11. We told him to assign the work to whoever was available. 11._____

12. Since John was the most efficient of any other employee in the bureau, he received the highest service rating. 12._____

13. Only those members of the national organization who resided in the middle West attended the conference in Chicago. 13._____

14. The question of whether the office manager has as yet attained, or indeed can ever hope to secure professional status is one which has been discussed for years. 14._____

15. No one knew who to blame for the error which, we later discovered, resulted in a considerable loss of time. 15._____

KEY (CORRECT ANSWERS)

1.	A	6.	B	11.	D
2.	A	7.	A	12.	A
3.	B	8.	C	13.	C
4.	B	9.	A	14.	B
5.	D	10.	D	15.	A

TEST 2

DIRECTIONS: Each of the sentences in this test may be classified under one of the following four categories:
- A. *Incorrect* because of faulty grammar or sentence structure
- B. *Incorrect* because of faulty punctuation
- C. *Incorrect* because of faulty capitalization
- D. *Correct*

1. The National alliance of Businessmen is trying to persuade private businesses to hire youth in the summertime.   1.____

2. The supervisor who is on vacation, is in charge of processing vouchers.   2.____

3. The activity of the committee at its conferences is always stimulating.   3.____

4. After checking the addresses again, the letters went to the mailroom.   4.____

5. The director, as well as the employees, are interested in sharing the dividends.   5.____

KEY (CORRECT ANSWERS)

1. C
2. B
3. D
4. A
5. A

TEST 3

DIRECTIONS: In each of the following groups of sentences, one of the four sentences is faulty in grammar, punctuation, or capitalization. Select the INCORRECT sentence in each case.

1. A. Sailing down the bay was a thrilling experience for me.
   B. He was not consulted about your joining the club.
   C. This story is different than the one I told you yesterday.
   D. There is no doubt about his being the best player.

   1._____

2. A. He maintains there is but one road to world peace.
   B. It is common knowledge that a child sees much he is not supposed to see.
   C. Much of the bitterness might have been avoided if arbitration had been resorted to earlier in the meeting.
   D. The man decided it would be advisable to marry a girl somewhat younger than him.

   2._____

3. A. In this book, the incident I liked least is where the hero tries to put out the forest fire.
   B. Learning a foreign language will undoubtedly give a person a better understanding of his mother tongue.
   C. His actions made us wonder what he planned to do next.
   D. Because of the war, we were unable to travel during the summer vacation.

   3._____

4. A. The class had no sooner become interested in the lesson than the dismissal bell rang.
   B. There is little agreement about the kind of world to be planned at the peace conference.
   C. "Today," said the teacher, "we shall read 'The Wind in the Willows,' I am sure you'll like it.
   D. The terms of the legal settlement of the family quarrel handicapped both sides for many years.

   4._____

5. A. I was so surprised that I was not able to say a word.
   B. She is taller than any other member of the class.
   C. It would be much more preferable if you were never seen in his company.
   D. We had no choice but to excuse her for being late.

   5._____

108

KEY (CORRECT ANSWERS)

1. C
2. D
3. A
4. C
5. C

TEST 4

DIRECTIONS: In each of the following groups of sentences, one of the four sentences is faulty in grammar, punctuation, or capitalization. Select the INCORRECT sentence in each case.

1. A. Please send me these data at the earliest opportunity.
   B. The loss of their material proved to be a severe handicap.
   C. My principal objection to this plan is that it is impracticable.
   D. The doll had laid in the rain for an hour and was ruined.

2. A. The garden scissors, left out all night in the rain, were in a badly rusted condition.
   B. The girls felt bad about the misunderstanding which had arisen
   C. Sitting near the campfire, the old man told John and I about many exciting adventures he had had.
   D. Neither of us is in a position to undertake a task of that magnitude.

3. A. The general concluded that one of the three roads would lead to the besieged city.
   B. The children didn't, as a rule, do hardly anything beyond what they were told to do.
   C. The reason the girl gave for her negligence was that she had acted on the spur of the moment.
   D. The daffodils and tulips look beautiful in that blue vase.

4. A. If I was ten years older, I should be interested in this work.
   B. Give the prize to whoever has drawn the best picture.
   C. When you have finished reading the book, take it back to the library.
   D. My drawing is as good as or better than yours.

5. A. He asked me whether the substance was animal or vegetable.
   B. An apple which is unripe should not be eaten by a child.
   C. That was an insult to me who am your friend.
   D. Some spy must of reported the matter to the enemy.

6. A. Limited time makes quoting the entire message impossible.
   B. Who did she say was going?
   C. The girls in your class have dressed more dolls this year than we.
   D. There was such a large amount of books on the floor that I couldn't find a place for my rocking chair.

7. A. What with his sleeplessness and his ill health, he was unable to assume any responsibility for the success of the meeting.
   B. If I had been born in February, I should be celebrating my birthday soon.
   C. In order to prevent breakage, she placed a sheet of paper between each of the plates when she packed them.
   D. After the spring shower, the violets smelled very sweet.

2 (#4)

8.
- A. He had laid the book down very reluctantly before the end of the lesson.
- B. The dog, I am sorry to say, had lain on the bed all night.
- C. The cloth was first lain on a flat surface; then it was pressed with a hot iron.
- D. While we were in Florida, we lay in the sun until we were noticeably tanned.

8.____

9.
- A. If John was in New York during the recent holiday season, I have no doubt he spent most of the time with his parents.
- B. How could he enjoy the television program; the dog was barking and the baby was crying.
- C. When the problem was explained to the class, he must have been asleep.
- D. She wished that her new dress were finished so that she could go to the party.

9.____

10.
- A. The engine not only furnishes power but light and heat as well.
- B. You're aware that we've forgotten whose guilt was established, aren't you?
- C. Everybody knows that the woman made many sacrifices for her children.
- D. A man with his dog and gun is a familiar sight in this neighborhood.

10.____

KEY (CORRECT ANSWERS)

1.	D	6.	D
2.	C	7.	B
3.	B	8.	C
4.	A	9.	B
5.	D	10.	A

TEST 5

DIRECTIONS: Each of Questions 1 through 5 consists of a sentence which may be classified appropriately under one of the following four categories:
A. *Incorrect* because of faulty grammar
B. *Incorrect* because of faulty punctuation
C. *Incorrect* because of faulty spelling
D. *Correct*

Examine each sentence carefully. Then, print in the space at the right the letter preceding the category which is the BEST of the four suggested above
(Note: Each incorrect sentence contains only one type of error. Consider a sentence correct if it contains no errors, although there may be other correct ways of writing the sentence.)

1. Of the two employees, the one in our office is the most efficient. 1.____

2. No one can apply or even understand, the new rules and regulations. 2.____

3. A large amount of supplies were stored in the empty office. 3.____

4. If an employee is occassionally asked to work overtime, he should do so willingly. 4.____

5. It is true that the new procedures are difficult to use but, we are certain that you will learn them quickly. 5.____

6. The office manager said that he did not know who would be given a large allotment under the new plan. 6.____

7. It was at the supervisor's request that the clerk agreed to postpone his vacation. 7.____

8. We do not believe that it is necessary for both he and the clerk to attend the conference. 8.____

9. All employees, who display perseverance, will be given adequate recognition. 9.____

10. He regrets that some of us employees are dissatisfied with our new assignments. 10.____

11. "Do you think that the raise was merited," asked the supervisor? 11.____

12. The new manual of procedure is a valuable supplament to our rules and regulations. 12.____

13. The typist admitted that she had attempted to pursuade the other employees to assist her in her work. 13.____

2 (#5)

14. The supervisor asked that all amendments to the regulations be handled by you and I. 14.____

15. The custodian seen the boy who broke the window. 15.____

KEY (CORRECT ANSWERS)

1. A	6. D	11. B
2. B	7. D	12. C
3. A	8. A	13. C
4. C	9. B	14. A
5. B	10. D	15. A

PREPARING WRITTEN MATERIAL
EXAMINATION SECTION
TEST 1

DIRECTIONS: Each short paragraph below is followed by four restatements or summaries of the information contained within it. Select the one that most completely and accurately restates the information given in the paragraph. *PRINT THE LETTER OF THE CORRECT ANSWER IN THE SPACE AT THE RIGHT.*

1. India's night jasmine, or hurshinghar, is different from most flowering plants, in that its flowers are closed during the day, and open after dark. The scientific reason for this is probably that the plant has avoided competing with other flowers for pollinating insects and birds, and relies instead on the service of nocturnal bats that are drawn to the flower's nectar. According to an old Indian legend, however, the flowers sprouted from the funeral ashes of a beautiful young girl who had fallen hopelessly in love with the sun.
   A. Despite the Indian legend that explains why the hurshinghar's flowers open at dusk, scientists believe it has to do with competition for available pollinators.
   B. The Indian hurshinghar's closure of its flowers during the day is due to a lack of available pollinators.
   C. The hurshinghar of India has evolved an unhealthy dependency on nocturnal bats.
   D. Like most myths, the Indian legend of the hurshinghar's night-flowering has been disproved by science.

1.____

2. Charles Lindbergh's trans-Atlantic flight from New York to Paris made him an international hero in 1927, but he lived nearly another fifty years, and by most accounts they weren't terribly happy ones. The two greatest tragedies of his life—the 1932 kidnapping and murder of his oldest son, and an unshakeable reputation as a Nazi sympathizer during World War II—he blamed squarely on the rabid media hounds who stalked his every move.
   A. Despite the fact that Charles Lindbergh had a hand in the two greatest tragedies of his life, he insisted on blaming the media for his problems.
   B. Charles Lindbergh lived a largely unhappy life after the glory of his 1927 trans-Atlantic flight, and he blamed his unhappiness on media attention
   C. Charles Lindbergh's later life was marked by despair and disillusionment.
   D. Because of the rabid media attention sparked by Charles Lindbergh's 1927 trans-Atlantic flight, he would later consider it the last happy event of his life

2.____

3. The United States, one of the world's youngest nations in the early twentieth century, had yet to spread its wings in terms of foreign affairs, preferring to remain isolated and opposed to meddling in the affairs of others. But the fact remained that as a young nation situated on the opposite side of the globe from Europe, Africa, and Asia, the United States had much work to do in

3.____

establishing relations with the rest of the world. So, too, as the European colonial powers continued to battle for influence in North and South America, did the United States come to believe that it was proper for them to keep these nations from encroaching into their sphere of influence.
- A. The roots of the Monroe Doctrine can be traced to the foreign policy shift of the United States during the early nineteenth century.
- B. In the early nineteenth century, the United States shifted its foreign policy to reflect a growing desire to actively protect its interests in the Western Hemisphere.
- C. In the early nineteenth century, the United States was too young and undeveloped to have devised much in the way of foreign policy.
- D. The United States adopted a more aggressive foreign policy in the early nineteenth century in order to become a diplomatic player on the world stage.

4. Hertha Ayrton, a nineteenth-century Englishwoman, pursued a career in science during a time when most women were not given the opportunity to go to college. Her series of successes led to her induction into the Institution of Electrical Engineers in 1899, when she was the first woman to receive this professional honor. Her most noted accomplishment was the research and invention of an anti-gas fan that the British War Office used in the trench warfare of World War I.
- A. The British Army's success in World War I can be partly attributed to Hertha Ayrton, a groundbreaking British scientist.
- B. Hertha Ayrton was the first woman to be inducted into the Institution of Electrical Engineers.
- C. The injustices of nineteenth-century England were no match for the brilliant mind of Hertha Ayrton.
- D. Hertha Ayrton defied the restrictions of her society by building a successful scientific career.

5. Scientists studying hyenas in Tanzania's Ngorongoro Crater have observed that hyena clans have evolved a system of territoriality that allows each clan a certain space to hunt within the 100-square-mile area. These territories are not marked by natural boundaries, but by droppings and excretions from the hyenas' scent glands. Usually, the hyenas take these boundary lines very seriously; some hyena clans have been observed abandoning their pursuit of certain prey after the prey has crossed into another territory, even though no members of the neighboring clan are anywhere in sight.
- A. The hyenas of Ngorongoro Crater illustrate that the best way to peacefully co-exist within a limited territory is to strictly delineate and defend territorial borders.
- B. While most territorial boundaries are marked using geographical features, the hyenas of Ngorongoro Crater have devised another method.
- C. The hyena clans of Ngorongoro Crater, in order to co-exist within a limited hunting territory, have developed a method of marking strict territorial boundaries.
- D. As with most species, the hyenas of Ngorongoro Crater have proven the age-old motto: "To the victor go the spoils."

3 (#1)

6. The flood control policy of the U.S. Army Corps of Engineers has long been an obvious feature of the American landscape—the Corps seeks to contain the nation's rivers with an enormous network of dams and levees, "channelizing" rivers into small, confined routes that will stay clear of settled flood—plains when rivers rise. As a command of the U.S. Army, the Corps seems to have long seen the nation's rivers as an enemy to be fought; one of the agency's early training films speaks of the Corps' "battle" with its adversary, Mother Nature.   6.____
    A. The dams and levees built by the U.S. Army Corps of Engineers have at least defeated their adversary, Mother Nature.
    B. The flood control policy of the U.S. Army Corps of Engineers has often reflected a military point of view, making the nation's rivers into enemies that must be defeated.
    C. When one realizes that the flood policy of the U.S. Army Corps of Engineers has always relied on a kind of military strategy, it is only possible to view the Corps' efforts as a failure.
    D. By damming and channelizing the nation's rivers, the U.S. Army Corps of Engineers have made America's flood plains safe for farming and development.

7. Frogs with extra legs or missing legs have been showing up with greater frequency over the past decade, and scientists have been baffled by the cause. Some researchers have concluded that pesticide runoff from farms is to blame; others say a common parasite, the trematode, is the culprit. Now, a new study suggests that both these factors in combination have disturbed normal development in many frogs, leading to the abnormalities.   7.____
    A. Despite several studies, scientists still have no idea what is causing the widespread incidence of deformities among aquatic frogs.
    B. In the debate over what is causing the increase in frog deformities, environmentalists tend to blame pesticide runoff, while others blame a common parasite, the trematode.
    C. A recent study suggests that both pesticide runoff and natural parasites have contributed to the increasing rate of deformities in frogs.
    D. Because of their aquatic habitat, frogs are among the most susceptible organisms to chemical ad environmental change, and this is illustrated by the increasing rate of physical deformities among frog populations.

8. The builders of the Egyptian pyramids, to insure that each massive structure was built on a completely flat surface, began by cutting a network of criss-crossing channels into the pyramid's mapped-out ground space and partly filling the channels with water. Because the channels were all interconnected, the water was distributed evenly throughout the channel system, and all the workers had to do to level their building surface was cut away any rock above the waterline.   8.____
    A. The modern carpenter's level uses a principle that was actually invented several centuries ago by the builders of the Egyptian pyramids.
    B. The discovery of the ancient Egyptians' sophisticated construction techniques is a quiet argument against the idea that they were built by slaves.

C. The use of water to insure that the pyramids were level mark the Egyptians as one of the most scientifically advanced of the ancient civilizations.
D. The builders of the Egyptian pyramids used a simple but ingenious method for ensuring a level building surface with interconnected channels of water

9. Thunderhead Mountain, a six-hundred-foot-high formation of granite in the Black Hills of South Dakota, is slowly undergoing a transformation that will not be finished for more than a century, when what remains of the mountain will have become the largest sculpture in the world. The statue, begun in 1947 by a Boston Sculptor named Henry Ziolkowski, is still being carved and blasted by his wife and children into the likeness of Crazy Horse, the legendary chief of the Sioux tribe of American natives. The enormity of the sculpture—the planned length of one of the figure's arms is 263 feet—is understandable, given the historical greatness of Crazy Horse.   9.____
    A. Only a hero as great as Crazy Horse could warrant a sculpture so large that it will take morae than a century to complete.
    B. In 1947, sculptor Henry Ziolkowski began work on what he imagined would be the largest sculpture in the world—even though he knew he would not live to see it completed.
    C. The huge Black Hills sculpture of the great Sioux chief Crazy Horse, still being carried out by the family of Henry Ziolkowski, will some day be the largest sculpture in the world.
    D. South Dakota's Thunderhead Mountain will soon be the site of the world's largest sculpture, a statue of the Sioux chief Crazy Horse.

10. Because they were some of the first explorers to venture into the western frontier of North America, the French were responsible for the naming of several native tribes. Some of these names were poorly conceived—the worst of which was perhaps Eskimo, the name for the natives of the far North, which translates roughly as "eaters of raw flesh." The name is incorrect; these people have always cooked their fish and game, and they now call themselves the Inuit, a native term that means "the people."   10.____
    A. The first to explore much of North America's western frontier were the French, and they usually gave improper or poorly-informed names to the native tribes.
    B. The Eskimos of North America have never eaten raw flesh, so it is curious that the French would give them a name that means "eaters of raw flesh."
    C. The Inuit have fought for many years to overcome the impression that they eat raw flesh.
    D. Like many native tribes, the Inuit were once incorrectly named by French explorers, but they have since corrected the mistake themselves.

5 (#1)

11. Of the 30,000 species of spiders worldwide, only a handful are dangerous to human beings, but this doesn't prevent many people from having a powerful fear of all spiders, whether they are venomous or not. The leading scientific theory about arachnophobia, as this fear is known, is that far in our evolutionary past, some species of spider must have presented a serious enough threat to people that the sight of a star-shaped body or an eight-legged walk was coded into our genes as a danger signal. 11.____
    A. Scientists theorize that peoples' widespread fear of spiders can be traced to an ancient spider species that was dangerous enough to trigger this fearful reaction.
    B. The fear known as arachnophobia is triggered by the sight of a star-shaped body or an eight-legged walk.
    C. Because most spiders have a uniquely shaped body that triggers a human fear response, many humans are afflicted with the fear of spiders known as arachnophobia.
    D. Though only a few of the planet's 30,000 spider species are dangerous to people, many people have an unreasonable fear of them.

12. From the 1970s to the 1990s, the percentage of Americans living in the suburbs climbed from 37% to 47%. In the latter part of the 1990s, a movement emerged that questioned the good of such a population shift—or at least, the good of the speed and manner in which this suburban land was being developed. Often, people began to argue, the planning of such growth was flawed, resulting in a phenomenon that has become known as suburban "sprawl," or the growth of suburban orbits around cities at rates faster than infrastructures could support, and in ways that are damaging to the environment 12.____
    A. The term "urban sprawl" was coined in the 1990s, when the movement against unchecked suburban development began to gather momentum.
    B. In the 1980s and 1990s, home builders benefited from a boom in their most favored demographic segment, suburban new home buyers.
    C. Suburban development tends to suffer from poor planning, which can lead to a lower quality of life for residents
    D. The surge in suburban residences in the late twentieth century was criticized by many as "sprawl" that could not be supported by existing resources

13. Medicare, a $200 billion-a-year program, processes 1 billion claims annually, and in the year 2000, the computer system that handles these claims came under criticism. The General Accounting Office branded Medicare's financial management system as outdated and inadequate—one in a series of studies and reports warning that the program is plagued with duplication, overcharges, double billings, and confusion among users. 13.____
    A. The General Accounting Office's 2000 report proves that Medicare is bloated bureaucracy in need of substantial reform.
    B. Medicare's confusing computer network is an example of how the federal government often neglects the programs that mean the most to average American citizens.

6 (#1)

    C. In the year 2000, the General Accounting Office criticized Medicare's financial accounting network as inefficient and outdated.
    D. Because it has to handle so many claims each year, Medicare's financial accounting system often produces redundancies and errors.

14. The earliest known writing materials were thin clay tablets, used in Mesopotamia more than 5,000 years ago. Although the tablets were cheap and easy to produce, they had two major disadvantages: they were difficult to store, and once the clay had dried and hardened, a person could not write on them. The ancient Egyptians later discovered a better writing material—the thin bark of the papyrus reed, a plant that grew near the mouth of the Nile River, which could be peeled into long strips, woven into a mat-like layer, pounded flat with heavy mallets, and then dried in the sun.   14.____
    A. The Egyptians, after centuries of frustration with clay writing tablets, were finally forced to invent a better writing surface.
    B. With the bark of the papyrus reed, ancient Egyptians made a writing material that overcame the disadvantages of clay tablets.
    C. The Egyptian invention of the papyrus scroll was necessitated in part by a relative lack of available clay.
    D. The word "paper" can be traced to the innovations of the Egyptians, who made the first paper-like writing material from the bark of papyrus plant.

15. In 1850, the German pianomaker Heinrich Steinweg and his family stepped off an immigrant ship in New York City, threw themselves into competition with dozens of other established craftsmen, and defeated them all by reinventing the instrument. The company they created commanded the market for nearly the next century and a half, while their competitors—some of the most acclaimed pianomakers in the business—faded into obscurity. And all the while, Steinway & Sons, through their sponsorship and encouragement of the world's most distinguished pianists, helped define the cultural life of the young United States.   15.____
    A. The Steinways capitalized on weak competition during the mid-nineteenth century to capture the American piano market.
    B. Because of their technical and cultural innovations, the Steinways had an advantage over other American pianomakers.
    C. Heinrich Steinweg founded the Steinway piano empire in 1850.
    D. From humble immigrant origins, the Steinway family rose to dominate both the pianomaking industry and American musical culture.

16. Feng Shui, the ancient Chinese science of studying the natural environment's effect on a person's well-being, has gained new popularity in the design and decoration of buildings. Although a complex area of study, a basic premise of Feng Shui is that each building creates a unique field of energy which affects the inhabitants of that building or home. In recent years, decorators and realtors have begun to offer services which include a diagnosis of a building's Feng Shui, or energy.   16.____
    A. Feng Shui, the Chinese science of balancing environmental energies, has been given more aesthetic quality by recent practitioners.

B. Generally, practitioners of Feng Shui work to create balance within a room, carefully arranging sharp and soft surfaces to create a positive environment that suits the room's primary purpose.
C. The idea behind the Chinese "science" of Feng Sui objects give off certain energies that affect a building's inhabitants has been a difficult one for most Westerners to accept, but it is gaining in popularity.
D. The ancient Chinese science of Feng Shui, which studies the balance of energies in a person's environment, has become popular among those who design and decorate buildings.

17. Because the harsh seasonal variations of the Kansas plains make survival difficult for most plant life, the area is dominated by tall, sturdy grasses. The only tree that has been able to survive and prosper throughout the wide expanse of prairie is the cottonwood, which can take root and grow in the most extreme climatic conditions. Sometimes a storm will shear off a living branch and carry it downstream, where it may snag along a sandbar and take root.   17.____
    A. Among the plant life of the Kansas plains, the only tree is the cottonwood.
    B. The only prosperous tree on the Kansas plains is the cottonwood, which can take root and grow in a wide range of conditions.
    C. Only the cottonwood, whose branches can grow after being broken off and washed down a river, is capable of surviving the climatic extremes of the Kansas plains.
    D. Because it is the most widespread and hardiest tree on the Kansas plains, the cottonwood had become a symbol of pioneer grit and fortitude.

18. In the twenty-first century, it's easy to see the automobile as the keystone of American popular culture. Subtract linen dusters, driving goggles, and women's *crepe de chine* veils from our history, and you've taken the Roaring out of the Twenties. Take away the ducktail haircuts, pegged pants, and upturned collars from the teen Car Cult of the Fifties, and the decade isn't nearly as Fabulous. Were the chromed and tailfinned muscle cars of the automobile' Golden Age modeled after us, or were we mimicking them?   18.____
    A. Ever since its invention, the automobile has shaped American culture.
    B. Many of the familiar names we give historical era, such as "Roaring Twenties" and "Fabulous Fifties," were given because of the predominance of the automobile.
    C. Americans' tastes in clothing have been determined primarily by the cars they drive.
    D. Teenagers have had a fascination for automobiles ever since the motorcar was first invented.

19. Since the 1960s, an important issue for Canada has been the status of minority French-speaking Canadians, especially in the province of Quebec, whose inhabitants make up 30% of the Canadian population and trace their ancestry back to a Canada that preceded British influence. In response to pressure from Quebec nationalists, the government in 1982 added a Charter of Rights to the constitution, restoring important rights that dated back to the time of aboriginal treaties. Separatism is still a prominent issue, though successive   19.____

referendums and constitutional inquiries have not resulted in any realistic progress toward Quebec's independence.
   A. Despite the fact that Quebec's inhabitants have their roots in Canada's original settlers, they have been constantly oppressed by the descendants of those who came later, the British.
   B. It seems unavoidable that Quebec's linguistic and cultural differences with the rest of Canada will some day lead to its secession.
   C. French-speaking Quebec's activism over the last several decades has led to concessions by the Canadian government, but it seems that Quebec will remain a part of the country for some time.
   D. The inhabitants of Quebec are an aboriginal culture that has been exploited by the Canadian government for years, but they are gradually winning back their rights.

20. For years, musicians and scientists have tried to discover what it is about an eighteenth-century Stradivarius violin—which may sell for more than $1 million on today's market—that gives it its unique sound. In 1977, American scientist Joseph Nagyvary discovered that the Stradivarius is made of a spruce wood that came from Venice, where timber was stored beneath the sea, and unlike the dry-seasoned wood from which other violins were made, this spruce contains microscopic holes which add resonance to the violin's sound. Nagyvary also found the varnish used on the Stradivarius to be equally unique, containing tiny mineral crystals that appear to have come from ground-up gemstones, which would filter out high-pitched tones and give the violin a smoother sound. 20.____
   A. After carefully studying Stradivarius violins to discover the source of their unique sound, an American scientist discovered two qualities in the construction of them that set them apart from other instruments: the wood from which they were made, and the varnish used to coat the wood.
   B. The two qualities that give the Stradivarius violin such a unique sound are the wood, which adds resonance, and the finish, which filters out high-pitched tones.
   C. The Stradivarius violin, because of the unique wood and finish used in its construction, is widely regarded as the finest string instrument ever manufactured in the world.
   D. A close study of the Stradivarius violin has revealed that the best wood for making violins is Venetian spruce, stored underwater.

21. People who watch the display of fireflies on a clear summer evening are actually witnessing a complex chemical reaction called "bioluminescence," which turns certain organisms into living light bulbs. Organisms that produce this light undergo a reaction in which oxygen combines with a chemical called lucerfin and an enzyme called luciferase. Depending on the organism, the light produced from this reaction can range from the light green of the firefly to the bright red spots of a railroad worm. 21.____
   A. Although the function of most displays of bioluminescence is to attract mates, as is the case with fireflies, other species rely on bioluminescence for different purposes.

B. Bioluminescence, a phenomenon produced by several organisms, is the result of a chemical reaction that takes place within the body of the organism.
C. Of all the organisms in the world, only insects are capable of displaying bioluminescence.
D. Despite the fact that some organisms display bioluminescence, these reactions produce almost no heat, which is why the light they create is sometimes referred to as cold light.

22. The first of America's "log cabin" presidents, Andrew Jackson rose from humble backcountry origins to become a U.S. congressman and senator, a renowned military hero, and the seventh president of the United States. Among many Americans, especially those of the western frontier, he was acclaimed as a symbol of the "new" American: self-made, strong through closeness to nature, and endowed with a powerful moral courage.   22.____
    A. Andrew Jackson was the first American president to rise from modest origins.
    B. Because he was born poor, President Andrew Jackson was more popular among Americans of the western frontier.
    C. Andrew Jackson's humble background, along with his outstanding achievements, made him into a symbol of American strength and self-sufficiency.
    D. Andrew Jackson achieved success as a legislator, soldier, and president because he was born humbly and had to work for every honor he ever received.

23. In the past few decades, while much of the world's imagination has focused on the possibilities of outer space, some scientists have been exploring a different frontier—the ocean floor. Although ships have been sailing the oceans for centuries, only recently have scientists developed vehicles strong enough to sustain the pressure of deep-sea exploration and observation. These fiberglass vehicles, called submersibles, are usually just big enough to take two or three people to the deepest parts of the oceans' floors.   23.____
    A. Modern submersible vehicles, thanks to recent technological innovations, are now exploring underwater cliffs, crevices, and mountain ranges that were once unreachable.
    B. While most people tend to fantasize about exploring outer space, they should be turning toward a more accessible realm—the depths of the earth's oceans.
    C. Because of the necessarily small size of submersible vehicles, exploration of the deep ocean is not a widespread activity.
    D. Recent technological developments have helped scientists to turn their attention from deep space to the deep ocean.

10 (#1)

24. The panda—a native of the remote mountainous regions of China—subsists almost entirely on the tender shoots of the bamboo plant. This restrictive diet has allowed the panda to evolve an anatomical structure that is completely different from that of other bears, whose paws are aligned for running, stabbing, and scratching. The panda's paw has an over-developed wrist bone that juts out below the other claws like a thumb, and the panda uses this "thumb" to grip bamboo shoots while it strips them of their leaves.
    A. The panda is the only bear-like animal that feeds on vegetation, and it has a kind of thumb to help it grip bamboo shoots.
    B. The panda's limited diet of bamboo has led it to evolve a thumb-like appendage for grasping bamboo shoots.
    C. The panda's thumb-like appendage is a factor that limits its diet to the shoots of the bamboo plant.
    D. Because bamboo shoots must be held tightly while eaten, the panda's thumb-like appendage ensure that it is the only bear-like animal that eats bamboo.

24.____

25. The stability and security of the Balkan region remains a primary concern for Greece in post-Cold War Europe, and Greece's active participation in peacekeeping and humanitarian operations in Georgia, Albania, and Bosnia are substantial examples of this commitment. Due to its geopolitical position, Greece believes it necessary to maintain, at least for now, a more nationalized defense force than other European nations. It is Greece's hope that the new spirit of integration and cooperation will help establish a common European foreign affairs and defense policy that might ease some of these regional tensions, and allow a greater level of Greek participation in NATO's integrated military structure.
    A. Greece's proximity to the unstable Balkan region has led it to keep a more nationalized military, though it hopes to become more involved in a common European defense force.
    B. The Balkan states present a greater threat to Greece than any other European nation, and Greece has adopted a highly nationalist military force as a result.
    C. Greece, the only Balkan state to belong to NATO, has an isolationist approach to defense, but hopes to achieve greater integration in the organization's combined forces.
    D. Greece's failure to become more militarily integrated with the rest of Europe can be attributed to the failure to establish a common European defense policy.

25.____

KEY (CORRECT ANSWERS)

1.	A	11.	A
2.	B	12.	D
3.	B	13.	C
4.	D	14.	B
5.	C	15.	D
6.	B	16.	D
7.	C	17.	B
8.	D	18.	A
9.	C	19.	C
10.	D	20.	A

21. B
22. C
23. D
24. B
25. A

PREPARING WRITTEN MATERIAL

PARAGRAPH REARRANGEMENT
COMMENTARY

The sentences that follow are in scrambled order. You are to rearrange them in proper order and indicate the letter choice containing the correct answer at the space at the right.

Each group of sentences in this section is actually a paragraph presented in scrambled order. Each sentence in the group has a place in that paragraph; no sentence is to be left out. You are to read each group of sentences and decide upon the best order in which to put the sentences so as to form a well-organized paragraph.

The questions in this section measure the ability to solve a problem when all the facts relevant to its solution are not given.

More specifically, certain positions of responsibility and authority require the employee to discover connection between events sometimes, apparently, unrelated. In order to do this, the employee will find it necessary to correctly infer that unspecified events have probably occurred or are likely to occur. This ability becomes especially important when action must be taken on incomplete information.

Accordingly, these questions require competitors to choose among several suggested alternatives, each of which presents a different sequential arrangement of the events. Competitors must choose the MOST logical of the suggested sequences.

In order to do so, they may be required to draw on general knowledge to infer missing concepts or events that are essential to sequencing the given events. Competitors should be careful to infer only what is essential to the sequence. The plausibility of the wrong alternatives will always require the inclusion of unlikely events or of additional chains of events which are NOT essential to sequencing the given events.

It's very important to remember that you are looking for the best of the four possible choices, and that the best choice of all may not even be one of the answers you're given to choose from.

There is no one right way to solve these problems. Many people have found it helpful to first write out the order of the sentences, as they would have arranged them, on their scrap paper before looking at the possible answers. If their optimum answer is there, this can save them some time. If it isn't, this method can still give insight into solving the problem. Others find it most helpful to just go through each of the possible choices, contrasting each as they go along. You should use whatever method feels comfortable and works for you.

While most of these types of questions are not that difficult, we've added a higher percentage of the difficult type, just to give you more practice. Usually there are only one or two questions on this section that contain such subtle distinctions that you're unable to answer confidently. And you then may find yourself stuck deciding between two possible choices, neither of which you're sure about.

PREPARING WRITTEN MATERIAL
PARAGRAPH REARRANGEMENT
EXAMINATION SECTION
TEST 1

DIRECTIONS: The sentences listed below are part of a meaningful paragraph, but they are not given in their proper order. You are to decide what would be the BEST order to put sentences to form a well-organized paragraph. Each sentence has a place in the paragraph; there are no extra sentences. *PRINT THE LETTER OF THE CORRECT ANSWER IN THE SPACE AT THE RIGHT.*

1.
   I. At first, I had very low enrollment, but then I started passing out flyers describing my services.
   II. Last summer I started a carwashing venture.
   III. I hope to save enough to buy my own carwash business one day.
   IV. I've been in business almost a year.
   V. After the advertising, I was booked every weekend during the summer.
   The CORRECT answer is:
   A. II, I, V, IV, III   B. I, II, IV, III, V   C. II, I, IV, V, III   D. V, III, IV, I, II

   1.____

2.
   I. Yesterday, John had to call work and tell them he wouldn't be able to come in.
   II. She wanted to eat at the new seafood restaurant in town.
   III. Two days ago, John and Sally went to dinner for Sally's birthday.
   IV. However, later John realized the sushi made him sick.
   V. They both tried the sushi and thought it tasted good.
   The CORRECT answer is:
   A. I, V, IV, III, II   B. III, II, V, IV, I   C. III, V, IV, I, II   D. V, IV, III, I, II

   2.____

3.
   I. Music programs should not be cut when school funds are tight.
   II. Some will argue that music programs are too costly.
   III. According to many experts, music programs have even shown the ability to re-engage student populations who have lost interest in scholastic endeavors.
   IV. There is a direct connection between school improvement and a student's connection to music.
   V. However, there are many different programs to choose from that are not as expensive.
   The CORRECT answer is:
   A. IV, II, V, I, III   B. I, III, IV, II, V   C. II, I, III, IV, V   D. I, IV, III, II, V

   3.____

4.
   I. The hockey team went undefeated in their tournament.
   II. Because the coach and their parents believed in them, the players played with great confidence.
   III. No one wanted to go home after they won the championship.
   IV. Their coach made them believe they could beat anyone they played.
   V. They were not expected to beat all of the teams in their bracket.
   The CORRECT answer is:
   A. III, II, V, IV, I   B. I, II, III, IV, V   C. I, V, IV, II, III   D. I, IV, V, II, III

   4.____

129

5. I.   The problem started when my alarm clock was set for 6:00 P.M. not 6:00 A.M., so I woke up late.
    II. I guess a neighbor's dog got loose before practice started, so it was delayed and no one notices I was a little tardy.
    III. I rode my bike as fast as I could and thought I was going to be in trouble for sure.
    IV. This morning was crazy because if I was late, I would get cut from the team.
    V.   When I got to the field, everyone was standing on the outside of the fence and there were policemen all on the field.
    The CORRECT answer is:
    A. I, IV, III, V, II   B. IV, III, I, II, V   C. I, V, II, III, IV   D. IV, I, III, V, II

6. I.   Lastly, do not eat food off of your date's plate unless they have offered it to you first.
    II. Do not tell jokes that aren't funny and especially do not laugh at them yourself.
    III. Remember, there are many ways to screw up a date, but these are the worst ways.
    IV. When on a first date, there are many ways to screw it up, but here are the three worst.
    V.   Do not forget to shower and groom yourself before showing up.
    The CORRECT answer is:
    A. IV, V, II, I, III   B. I, V, IV, II, III   C. IV, III, II, I, V   D. V, IV, II, I, III

7. I.   We could prevent drunk drivers from harming themselves or others by by providing this service.
    II. Thousands each year die because of accidents caused by drugs or alcohol.
    III. Many are not willing to pay for a taxi and decide to drive themselves home instead.
    IV. While the cost may be a burden to the wallet, it would be small compared to the loss of a loved one because of drunk driving.
    V.   Lives could be saved if the town started a free taxi service.
    The CORRECT answer is:
    A. I, III, V, IV, II   B. II, V, III, I, IV   C. II, III, I, V, IV   D. V, III, II, IV, I

8. I.   These amazing animals are disappearing at a startling rate.
    II. Do people really want to explain to our grandchildren why they can only see these majestic animals in a book?
    III. Zoos all across the country do not want the Siberian tiger to vanish.
    IV. We can also make donations to charities and sanctuaries that protect the Siberian tiger.
    V.   If we write to local governments, we could let them know we demand the preservation of this species.
    The CORRECT answer is:
    A. I, III, V, II, IV   B. V, II, I, III, IV   C. III, I, V, IV, II   D. II, IV, V, I, III

9. I. Often, they have been described as eating machines, and their design certainly matches perfectly for that activity.
    II. Of all the creatures that live in water, Orcas are the greediest eaters and killers.
    III. As soon as they finish a meal, Orcas are on the prowl for more food.
    IV. Orcas, better known as killer whales, are powerful swimmers, with sleek, muscled, stream-lined bodies.
    V. They suffer from continual hunger.
    The CORRECT answer is:
    A. II, V, III, I, IV   B. II, III, I, IV, V   C. V, II, III, IV, I   D. I, IV, II, III, V

10. I. Sleep researchers have recently concluded that high school students need more sleep than they currently get.
    II. In an attempt to aid high school students get more sleep, some schools have delayed start times so students can perform better.
    III. In addition to having difficulty with thinking, students who are sleep deprived often see more stress in their lives because of an increase in stress hormones like cortisol.
    IV. Consistent data has determined that sleep is necessary to help with creating memories and solving complex issues.
    V. At school, teens have difficulty with complex thought because many of them do not get enough sleep each night.
    The CORRECT answer is:
    A. I, V, III, II, IV   B. IV, III, I, V, II   C. I, IV, V, III, II   D. II, III, V, IV, I

11. I. It took me twice as long to pack because I was so excited.
    II. That all changed on the last day of school.
    III. Until last year, I had never been out of the state, let alone out of the country.
    IV. My sister decided to take me on a trip to London.
    V. Now I think I want to be a travel agent, so I can see the world.
    The CORRECT answer is:
    A. II, IV, I, V, III   B. III, II, IV, I, V   C. IV, V, I, III, II   D. III, IV, II, I, V

12. I. The owner felt that tattoos gave a negative image for the coffee shop.
    II. Furthermore, a clean cut appearance would attract better customers.
    III. Since then, the policy has seen few complaints from residents or employees.
    IV. In 2008, a coffee shop in Billings, Montana instituted a policy that banned employees from having tattoos that can be seen by customers.
    V. When one of the employees refused to wear a long sleeve shirt to cover up, he was told he could no longer work at the coffee shop.
    The CORRECT answer is:
    A. IV, II, III, I, V   B. V, I, II, IV, III   C. I, II, V, III, IV   D. IV, I, II, V, III

13.
   I. Our household might have been described as uncooperative.
   II. When the tide was high, she would be standing on the inlet bridge with her waders on.
   III. Everything was subservient to the disposal of the tides.
   IV. I grew up with buckets, shovels, and nets waiting by the back door.
   V. When the tide was low, Mom could be found down on the mudflats.
   The CORRECT answer is:
   A. I, V, IV, V, III   B. IV, I, III, V, II   C. V, IV, II, I, III   D. II, IV, I, III, V

14.
   I. A 2012 survey found that over 50% of those polled thought educators were prohibited from teaching about religion.
   II. The result is that many schools and teachers are hesitant to educate students about world religions.
   III. However, for many it is impossible to deny the role that religion plays in history and literature.
   IV. As many people know, the First Amendment guarantees the separation of church and state.
   V. Ultimately, this is a dilemma that will continue to plague Social Studies and World History educators.
   The CORRECT answer is:
   A. IV, I, III, V, II   B. I, III, V, II, IV   C. IV, III, II, I, V   D. II, III, V, IV, I

15.
   I. The Wampanoag religion was similar to that of the other Algonquin tribes.
   II. They also had spiritual beliefs about animals, and the forest.
   III. Then, they told their stories of the cycle of life and the Great Spirit.
   IV. They expressed their religious beliefs during festivals and at night when they sat at huge campfires.
   V. In those times, people believed in a Great Spirit and many other things that Nature had a part of the Great Spirit in them.
   The CORRECT answer is:
   A. I, V, II, IV, III   B. V, II, III, I, IV   C. I, II, III, IV, V   D. III, IV, II, V, I

16.
   I. Consumers spend an endless amount of money each year on cutting, lengthening, highlighting and curling hair.
   II. Brunettes want to be blonde, redheads long to be brunettes, and all cringe at the thought of gray hair.
   III. Why is everyone so obsessed with the hair on their heads?
   IV. These thoughts all crossed my mind as I examine the result of my most recent hair adventure.
   V. The result was not quite what I expected, but I resolved to live with it, as it's my hair and no one else's!
   The CORRECT answer is:
   A. I, IV, V, II, III   B. I, III, II, IV, V   C. IV, I, III, V, II   D. III, I, II, IV, V

17.   I.   It was only years afterwards that he learned his ancestors were actually accomplished coppersmiths.
      II. He's an old-fashioned current day blacksmith that still practices manipulating metal over hot fires.
      III. This started him on his quest to collect and read any and every book concerning the nature and process of blacksmithing.
      IV. Beginning at age 30, Lee's attraction to metal work lay in creating an object out of such obstinate material such as iron.
      V.   While one will probably never read about him in a history book, Mr. Amos Lee contributes mightily to the preservation of America.
      The CORRECT answer is:
      A. II, III, I, IV, V   B. V, II, IV, III, I   C. III, I, V, II, IV   D. I, IV, III, V, II

18.   I.   After she was stung, she killed the scorpion with a boot, and flushed it down the sink.
      II. My sister once told me about a scorpion that stung her in her bed.
      III. As she recounted her tale of horror, I could only wonder how she remained so calm.
      IV. Later, she realized she should've kept it to figure out what type of scorpion it was.
      V.   While she's lucky to be alive, it could've been a deadly scorpion that would've required medical attention immediately.
      The CORRECT answer is:
      A. II, III, I, IV, V   B. II, I, IV, V, III   C. I, IV, II, III, V   D. V, II, III, I, IV

19.   I.   While the majority of people know this, it was not always the case.
      II. Many laws hold sponsors responsible to participants and courts are full of non-compliance lawsuits on both sides.
      III. Seven months after departure, she arrived at her destination, battered and tired, but the contest sponsors were nowhere to be found.
      IV. For anyone who has ever entered a contest, the rules and disclaimers that go along with each one are well known.
      V.   In 1896, a contest motivated a Norwegian immigrant to travel from New York City to the state of Washington.
      The CORRECT answer is:
      A. II, III, V, IV, I   B. V, I, IV, III, II   C. IV, II, I, V, III   D. I, IV, III, II, V

20.   I.   One thought as to why this happens is due to a person's circadian rhythm being thrown off.
      II. While most people find traveling internationally to be exhilarating, those same people would probably agree that the worst part is the jet lag.
      III. It is considered a sleeping disorder, albeit one that is temporary and not as serious as other sleeping dysfunctions.
      IV. Normally, the body operates on a 24-hour time period in conjunction with the earth's 24-hour cycle of night and day.
      V.   When one adds or subtracts time while traveling, a condition known as desynchronosis likely affects them.
      The CORRECT answer is:
      A. I, II, III, IV, V   B. IV, I, III, V, II   C. III, IV, I, II, V   D. II, V, III, I, IV

21.
   I. The consumption rate is due to its ability to create cleaner fuel for electrical power.
   II. While cleaner burning fuel is optimal, the usage rate will mean the U.S. only has about a five-year supply of natural gas.
   III. Current research studies are showing that Americans use around 20 trillion cubic feet (TCF) on a yearly basis.
   IV. It is no wonder, then, that natural gas has become such a controversial and critical topic for politicians, businesses, and consumers.
   V. While gasoline is still a crucial energy source, natural gas actually supplies approximately one-fourth of America's energy needs.
   The CORRECT answer is:
   A. I, IV, II, III, V   B. IV, II, III, V, I   C. V, III, I, II, IV   D. III, V, IV, I, II

21.____

22.
   I. Their protection comes from bony plates covered by leathery skin.
   II. This desert wanderer has few worries and one can understand why: his "coat" of armor.
   III. What would be certain death for most animals, armadillos meander along highway shoulders and remains surprisingly unaffected.
   IV. While their shells are not impenetrable, the armadillo can relax knowing that he is safer than many animals who wander the roads of the southwest.
   V. While on the smaller side, armadillos are equipped to deal with aggressive and dangerous predators.
   The CORRECT answer is:
   A. III, II, V, I, IV   B. IV, I, II, V, III   C. I, III, IV, II, V   D. V, IV, I, III, II

22.____

23.
   I. Since its discovery in 1930, Pluto has had a troubled history concerning its acceptance as a planet.
   II. Anytime there is a controversial topic like this, it is sure to be debated for years to come.
   III. Some researchers believe that it is a planet arguing that Pluto is almost 1,000 times bigger than an average comet.
   IV. However, others argue that due to its icy composition and irregular orbit, Pluto more likely belongs to the Kuiper Belt, which features sizeable comets.
   V. They also argue that any would be planet must be large enough to be pulled into a spherical shape by its own gravity, which like the other eight, Pluto can lay claim to.
   The CORRECT answer is:
   A. IV, V, I, II, III   B. I, III, V, IV, II   C. III, I, IV, V, II   D. II, IV, V, III, I

23.____

24.
   I. When I found out I'd be traveling to France, I was so ecstatic.
   II. He told me that studying may be difficult because I will want to meet new friends and see all the landmarks associated with such a beautiful country.
   III. My brother has also been in an exchange before and he had some advice for me.
   IV. Despite his warnings to study hard, I know I would be disappointed if I didn't do any sightseeing at all.
   V. In the fall, I will be participating in a foreign exchange program.
   The CORRECT answer is:
   A. I, V, II, IV, III   B. IV, II, I, III, V   C. III, I, II, IV, IV   D. V, I, III, II, IV

25.
   I. Well over two hundred years ago, Lewis and Clark set forth on a journey at the request of President Thomas Jefferson.
   II. Their instructions were simple; they needed to find the fastest route across North America.
   III. Throughout it all, including long winters and harsh conditions, the travelers forged west in search of a trade route using only rivers.
   IV. The actual task was much more difficult as it would require them to set a course through dangerous territories replete with hostile natives and ferocious animals.
   V. While land travel ended up being faster, many still credit this group with "breaking through" into the unknown land and launching a movement for westward expansion.
   The CORRECT answer is:
   A. I, II, IV, III, V   B. II, I, III, IV, V   C. V, III, IV, II, I   D. IV, I, III, V, II

8 (#1)

KEY (CORRECT ANSWERS)

1.	A	11.	B
2.	B	12.	D
3.	D	13.	B
4.	C	14.	C
5.	D	15.	A
6.	A	16.	D
7.	B	17.	B
8.	C	18.	A
9.	A	19.	C
10.	C	20.	D

21. C
22. A
23. B
24. D
25. A

TEST 2

DIRECTIONS: The sentences listed below are part of a meaningful paragraph, but they are not given in their proper order. You are to decide what would be the BEST order to put sentences to form a well-organized paragraph. Each sentence has a place in the paragraph; there are no extra sentences. *PRINT THE LETTER OF THE CORRECT ANSWER IN THE SPACE AT THE RIGHT.*

1.
   I. Whenever I start to feel sadness and disgust over a poor hair style, I ask myself why we are so obsessed with the hair on our heads.
   II. The answer always comes to me in a flash.
   III. Soon after this realization, I often cease my crying over how I look.
   IV. It's pure vanity; no other reason explains fully why we worry about how to style, color or cut our follicles.
   V. Instead, I focus on positive, kind thoughts towards myself and others, which usually allows me to overcome any negative feelings I had right after I looked in the mirror.
   The CORRECT answer is:
   A. III, I, V, IV, II   B. I, II, IV, III, V   C. IV, III, II, V, I   D. V, IV, I, II, III

   1.____

2.
   I. The riverboat director was our captain and our host.
   II. We affectionately watched him with his back toward us, as he stood at the helm, looking toward the sea.
   III. Within all of the Mississippi River, nothing looked nearly as nautical and trustworthy as our pilot as he surveyed the waters before him.
   IV. What we had not realized at the time was that his work was not out there in the estuaries, but rather behind him, within the gloom of the vessel.
   V. We would realize soon enough, however, how difficult the next few days would get, and why he was so ponderous on that ship deck.
   The CORRECT answer is:
   A. III, I, IV, II, V   B. IV, II, III, V, I   C. V, II, I, IV, III   D. I, III, II, IV, V

   2.____

3.
   I. Ultimately, no new qualities are added to an object, person, or action when it becomes good.
   II. Whenever one examines the word "good", there is always an implied end to be reached.
   III. The good is useful, and it must be used for something.
   IV. However, good is a relative term.
   V. So in that light, whether good is spoken out loud or silently assumed, it is a mental exercise to something else that puts all meaning into it.
   The CORRECT answer is:
   A. V, II, I, IV, III   B. III, I, V, II, IV   C. I, V, IV, III, II   D. II, IV, III, V, I

   3.____

4.
I. There are specific temperature ranges for petroleum gas, kerosene, oil stocks and also residue.
II. Called fractional distillation, the oil is heated and drawn off at different points, which leads to the various products.
III. To start, the oil is heated up to around 600 degrees Celsius, which vaporizes it.
IV. From there, the vapors cool and condense as they move upwards and eventually turn back into liquid and flows into various tanks.
V. Crude oil is refined when it is split into different by-products.
The CORRECT answer is:
A. II, III, I, V, IV   B. IV, I, IV, III, V   C. V, II, I, III, IV   D. I, IV, II, III, V

4._____

5.
I. With that said, x-ray distortion has more than one use regarding planets.
II. The higher "bend" in an x-ray would seemingly indicate a larger planet, while lower bending would most likely mean a smaller planet.
III. Distortion can also help determine how a planet orbits its star.
IV. Releasing x-rays by distant stars can help reveal the presence of planets orbiting these stars.
V. The distortion of the x-rays, which is how scientists would tell if planets are near, would be caused by gravitational pull exerted from planets.
The CORRECT answer is:
A. IV, V, II, I, III   B. V, IV, III, I, II   C. II, III, I, IV, V   D. I, V, II, III, IV

5._____

6.
I. Some feel that this fact reflects the rise of English as an accepted language of business around the world, and, therefore, that foreign languages are lessening in importance.
II. Foreign language instruction is dropping in U.S. public high schools.
III. They feel that this drop is actually a threat to the nation's vitality in what is an ever-increasing multicultural marketplace.
IV. Others feel that the reduction in language study is a U.S. failure to integrate with the rest of the world.
V. The question then becomes this, should greater support be given to foreign language programs in U.S. public schools?
The CORRECT answer is:
A. V, IV, III, I, II   B. III, IV, V, II, I   C. II, I, IV, III, V   D. IV, II, III, V, I

6._____

7.
I. The owner, Nate, still runs the joint, which means it doesn't usually close until he's served the last customer.
II. The alley might dissuade visitors from finding this local gem, but if one can get past the masking tape and yellowing paint that line the door, they will be in for a real treat.
III. The Shack, as the locals call it, is located in a nondescript alley across from beautiful City Park.
IV. While I'd love for Nate to get more publicity, I'm just fine with knowing that the Shack will have a short line and a great ambience each time I stop in.
V. Nathan's Crab Shack serves up some of the best sandwiches I've ever eaten.
The CORRECT answer is:
A. III, II, V, IV, I   B. I, IV, II, III, V   C. II, V, I, IV, III   D. V, I, III, II, IV

7._____

8. I. All activity halted, however, at the onset of World War II, so construction did not officially begin until the early 1950s.
    II. In total, it took almost three years to build, cost five men their lives, and cost the state of Michigan more than $40 million.
    III. In the 1930's, the Mackinac Bridge Authority sought funding from the federal government to construct a bridge.
    IV. Even though they were denied, the MBA plotted a route and studied the lake bed and rock below.
    V. Despite numerous setbacks, the Mackinac Bridge opened to traffic on November 1, 1957, and for years it was the longest suspension bridge in the world.
    The CORRECT answer is:
    A. II, I, V, IV, III   B. III, IV, I, II, V   C. V, III, IV, I, II   D. I, II, III, V, IV

8.____

9. I. It also teaches them to bargain and trade for cards to complete their sets.
    II. Collecting cards is a rewarding experience not only for kids, but also adults.
    III. It teaches important skills, such as patience and organization.
    IV. Lastly, card collecting is a social activity that encourages the old and the young to swap stories, cards, and knowledge in a fun and engaging way.
    V. For younger collectors, it enhances fine motor skills such as developing a more careful touch.
    The CORRECT answer is:
    A. III, IV, I, II, V   B. II, V, III, IV, I   C. I, II, V, III, IV   D. II, III, V, I, IV

9.____

10. I. Spyware can cripple unsecured computers and data around the world.
    II. Even when computer users experience program crashes and warnings about missing system files, they tend to wait until these problems get too ad to manage.
    III. Sometimes it is used for marketing agencies, but just as often there is a more malicious intent behind spyware stored on an unsecured computer.
    IV. Much of the time, the cause of these problems rests with the biggest online threat there is: spyware.
    V. While most people do not realize it, those who use a personal computer to connect to the internet expose themselves to many risks.
    The CORRECT answer is:
    A. II, IV, V, III, I   B. V, II, IV, I, III   C. III, II, I, IV, V   D. V, IV, I, II, III

10.____

11. I. When people have parties at their homes, Susan cooks for them, and she is a fabulous cook.
    II. My friend, Susan, owns her own catering business.
    III. Once everything has been planned, Susan will hire servers to wait on the people.
    IV. One of the things that makes her so good is that she asks the customer lots of questions like how many people will be there and what food the customer would like to serve.
    V. All in all, she loves the work involved with her catering business and it does not hurt that she's really good at it.

11.____

The CORRECT answer is:
A. II, I, IV, III, V   B. I, III, V, II, IV   C. IV, II, I, III, V   D. V, IV, I, III, II

12.
I. "To be, or not to be...." is an extremely well-known phrase that has been the source of both mystery and wonderment since the turn of the 16th century.
II. Where did it come from and what does it mean?
III. As for the meaning of the phrase, a complete answer would necessitate a deeper, more comprehensive look into Shakespeare culture and nuance.
IV. The first question is easy enough to answer: from Shakespeare's famous play, *Hamlet*.
V. The issue, however, is that despite the fact that everyone knows the phrase, few actually know the context of this well-worn saying.
The CORRECT answer is:
A. V, I, III, II, IV   B. II, III, IV, V, I   C. I, V, II, IV, III   D. IV, II, I, III, V

12.____

13.
I. For example, it was recently discovered that we were connected to a Civil War ancestor that we previously had not known about.
II. He maintains the records of births, deaths, marriages, and even divorces, and he takes the job very seriously.
III. This ancestor bestowed his beautiful and antique furniture to his children, who then passed the items down to their descendants.
IV. My Uncle Mike is the genealogist of our family.
V. In fact, he will even send out letters to our family whenever something noteworthy occurs.
The CORRECT answer is:
A. II, III, I, IV, V   B. V, IV, II, III, I   C. I, II, IV, V, III   D. IV, II, V, I, III

13.____

14.
I. He was part of a team that performed complicated experiments during the 1940s.
II. However, he is most likely known for his creation of "Murphy's Law."
III. While many Americans do not know the name Edward Murphy, they owe a considerable debt to this member of the Air Force.
IV. This somewhat funny observation has actually inspired similar "laws" such as Hofstadter's Law.
V. This "law" states that "if anything can go wrong, it will."
The CORRECT answer is:
A. I, III, V, II, IV   B. III, IV, V, I, II   C. III, I, II, V, IV   D. V, II, IV, I, III

14.____

15.
I. During winter months, its white coat is ideal to camouflage and the insulation provided by its unbeatable fur lining allows the fox to hunt all winter long.
II. While this strategy could be fruitful, it also carries risk because of the possibility that the polar bear might consume the fox if it catches it.
III. One of the Snow Fox's unique traits is the ability to adapt to extreme weather conditions.

15.____

IV. When food becomes scarce, the Arctic fox can follow polar bears as they attack seals on the sea ice.
V. Often referred to as the "Snow Fox," the Arctic fox is comparable in size to a domestic cat.
The CORRECT answer is:
A. V, III, I, IV, II B. II, IV, III, I, V C. III, I, V, II, IV D. IV, III, II, V, I

16.
I. The venerable professor, aged 85, encouraged his audience to show compassion for the poor and homeless in the city.
II. Students flocked to hear the returning professor, Dr. Willis, give a speech.
III. He abhors opulence and urges people to be charitable through frugality.
IV. Dr. Willis, a kind and empathetic activist for the poor, spoke to a full auditorium on Tuesday.
V. Much of his work is due to his personal memories stemming from the Great Depression.
The CORRECT answer is:
A. I, II, III, IV, V B. V, IV, III, II, I C. III, I, IV, II, V D. II, IV, I, V, III

16.____

17.
I. As some of his friends have noted, this antisocial attitude is an aberration for him, as he is normally quite extroverted and cheerful.
II. Many people have tried to evoke some of his normal geniality, but it has not worked, which is disconcerting.
III. It is now a commonly held belief that the only antidote to Johnny's stressful situation would be complete and total success on his exam.
IV. Upon learning of his pending exam, his roommates have agreed that his current mood is directly correlated to the test.
V. Upon being informed of an upcoming test in statistics, Johnny has started to act aloof and uninterested in social activities.
The CORRECT answer is:
A. I, V, II, III, IV B. IV, III, I, V, II C. II, IV, I, III, V D. V, I, IV, II, III

17.____

18.
I. When viewing a star formation through the Spitzer Space Telescope, a person has a view of disruption.
II. The Spitzer Space Telescope challenges the commonly held thought that smooth gas clouds gracefully facilitate the creation of new stars.
III. The relative few stars can be attributed to the turbulence that these processes bring to the heavens.
IV. Through the telescope's lens, one can see the creation of a star that disrupts nearby space.
V. Recent models of star formation, aided by telescopes like Spitzer, recognize that stars interact with one another in their stellar neighborhood.
The CORRECT answer is:
A. IV, II, I, III, V B. I, IV, II, V, III C. III, I, V, IV, II D. II, V, III, I, IV

18.____

19. I. In addition, models predicting the placement of electrons within the cloud describe one probability among many, instead of showing planet-like electrons orbiting a sun-like nucleus.
    II. Although the majority of us think of an atom's nucleus being orbited by electrons, the reality differs considerably from the stereotypical depiction.
    III. Oddly enough, it is mostly composed of empty space: its nucleus, made of protons and neutrons, makes up only about a billionth of the atom itself.
    IV. As many people know, the atom is the basic building block of matter.
    V. Researchers prefer to describe the electron movement as a "wave-pattern cloud."
    The CORRECT answer is:
    A. III, I, V, IV, II   B. V, III, IV, I, II   C. IV, III, II, V, I   D. II, V, I, III, IV

19.____

20. I. These buildings were thought to have been constructed upwards in order to thwart would-be attackers.
    II. Ancient Yemeni architects created a walled city that they called Shibam.
    III. Nowadays, with the planning of mile-high skyscrapers planned for construction, Shibam does not seem as impressive, but given their tools and knowledge at the time, the city will be held in esteem in architecturfal history books.
    IV. This wonder of the old world is now dubbed "Manhattan of the Desert".
    V. The city was composed of 500 buildings, ranging from five to eight stories high.
    The CORRECT answer is:
    A. II, IV, V, I, III   B. V, III, I, IV, II   C. IV, V, II, III, I   D. III, I, IV, II, V

20.____

21. I. Almost 2,000 years after being buried by falling ash from a volcanic eruption, the residents of Pompeii do reveal fascinating details about daily life in the Roman Empire.
    II. Pompeii's population, roughly 20,000 inhabitants, practiced several different religions.
    III. This is evidenced by temples dedicated to Egyptian gods, as well as Jewish temples and worshippers of Cybele.
    IV. While radically different in beliefs, Pompeii's citizens practiced all of these religions in peaceful co-existence with followers of the state religion.
    V. These people worshipped Jupiter and the Roman emperor.
    The CORRECT answer is:
    A. I, III, V, II, IV   B. II, IV, I, III, V   C. IV, I, III, V, II   D. III, II, IV, I, V

21.____

22.
   I. Instead of driving there, I may just stay home and cook myself a big breakfast with toast, fruit, eggs, and bacon.
   II. I was going to take a jog around the neighborhood to train for my race.
   III. As I woke up today, I realized that it would be yet another rainy day.
   IV. Now, I will have to drive to the gymnasium that is on the opposite side of town.
   V. After I eat, hopefully the rain will have gone away so I can train successfully.
   The CORRECT answer is:
   A. IV, I, II, V, III   B. III, II, IV, I, V   C. II, IV, I, III, V   D. V, III, II, I, IV

   22.____

23.
   I. Yesterday, he received a call from an H.R. representative of a firm in Chicago.
   II. The H.R. rep asked William to fly out to Chicago for an interview and he even offered to pay for William's plane ticket.
   III. Having received such a generous offer, William could not say no to the interview.
   IV. The interview will take place in one week, so William will spend the next few days researching the company's history.
   V. William has been searching for a full-time job for the last few months.
   The CORRECT answer is:
   A. IV, II, III, I, V   B. V, II, I, IV, III   C. I, II, III, IV, V   D. V, I, II, III, IV

   23.____

24.
   I. I wonder when I'll feel well enough to go back to work.
   II. I've tried eating chicken soup, drinking orange juice, taking Benadryl since the weekend.
   III. I finally decided to visit the doctor to see if I can get any stronger medicine to help me.
   IV. My allergies have been terrible the last several days.
   V. I've been blowing my nose, sneezing, and coughing the entire time.
   The CORRECT answer is:
   A. V, II, IV, III, I   B. I, III, II, IV, V   C. IV, V, II, III, I   D. II, III, V, I, IV

   24.____

25.
   I. Myrta is a sophomore in college and she's working on her degree in Special Education.
   II. In order to prepare herself for her career, she works at a camp in the summer.
   III. All of the children who attend this camp have physical and mental disabilities.
   IV. Myrta helps the kids get exercise and increase their social skills.
   V. At the end of each summer, she cannot wait to start her career in Special Education.
   The CORRECT answer is:
   A. V, I, II, III, IV   B. I, II, III, IV, V   C. III, IV, V, I, II   D. V, IV, III, II, I

   25.____

KEY (CORRECT ANSWERS)

1.	B	11.	A
2.	A	12.	C
3.	D	13.	D
4.	C	14.	C
5.	A	15.	A
6.	C	16.	D
7.	D	17.	D
8.	B	18.	B
9.	D	19.	C
10.	B	20.	A

21. A
22. B
23. D
24. C
25. B

PREPARING WRITTEN MATERIAL
PARAGRAPH REARRANGEMENT

EXAMINATION SECTION
TEST 1

DIRECTIONS: The sentences listed below are part of a meaningful paragraph, but they are not given in their proper order. You are to decide what would be the BEST order to put sentences to form a well-organized paragraph. Each sentence has a place in the paragraph; there are no extra sentences. *PRINT THE LETTER OF THE CORRECT ANSWER IN THE SPACE AT THE RIGHT.*

Questions 1-3.

DIRECTIONS: Questions 1 through 3 are to be answered on the basis of the following paragraph.

The CDC estimates that food-borne pathogens cause approximately 48 million illnesses, 3,000 deaths, and 128,000 hospitalizations in the United States each year. Contamination with disease-causing microbes called pathogens is usually due to improper food handling or storage. Other causes of food-borne diseases are toxic chemicals or other harmful substances in food and beverages. Food-borne diseases are illnesses caused when people consume contaminated food or beverages. More than 250 food-borne illnesses have been described, according to the United States Centers for Disease Control and Prevention (CDC).

1. When the five sentences are arranged in proper order, the paragraph starts with the sentence that begins:
    A. "Food-borne diseases..."
    B. "More than 250..."
    C. "Other causes of..."
    D. The CDC estimates..."

1.____

2. If the above paragraph were correctly organized, which of the following transition words would be appropriate to place at the beginning of the sentence that starts "The CDC estimates..."?
    A. With that said
    B. However
    C. To start off
    D. Ultimately

2.____

3. When the above paragraph is properly arranged, it ends with the words:
    A. "...Disease Control and Prevention (CDC).
    B. "...improper food handling or storage."
    C. "...United States each year."
    D. "...in food and beverages."

3.____

Questions 4-7.

DIRECTIONS: Questions 4 through 7 are to be answered on the basis of the following passage.

145

Her father, Abraham Quintanilla, who worked in the shipping department of a chemical plant and later opened a restaurant, had fronted a moderately successful band called Los Dinos ("The Guys") as a young man. Among them, her murder evoked an outpouring of grief comparable to that experienced by other Americans after the deaths of such major cultural figures as President John F. Kennedy. Selena had become an icon in the Hispanic community.

Selena Quintanilla was born in Lake Jackson, Texas, near Houston, on April 16, 1971. She had turned into a beloved figure to whom Mexican-Americans attached their aspirations and their feelings about their cultural identities. The violent death of beloved Tejano vocalist Selena on Mach 31, 1995 brought to an end more than just a promising musical career.

4. When arranged properly, the paragraph's opening sentence should start with: 4._____
    A. "Among them…" B. "The violent death…"
    C. "Her father, Abraham…" D. "Selena had become…"

5. In the second sentence listed above, "them" refers to 5._____
    A. Selena and her fans B. other non-Mexican Americans
    C. Selena and John F. Kennedy D. Mexican-Americans

6. After correctly organizing the paragraph, the author decides to split it into two separate paragraphs. Which of the following would begin the newly made second paragraph? 6._____
    A. "Selena had become…" B. "Selena Quintanilla was…"
    C. "The violent death…" D. "Her father, Abraham…"

7. When correctly organized, the final sentence of the paragraph should end end with the words: 7._____
    A. "…as a young man." B. "…on April 16, 1971."
    C. "…in the Hispanic community." D. "…a promising music career."

Questions 8-10.

DIRECTIONS: Questions 8 through 10 are to be answered on the basis of the following paragraph.

Whether Death takes the form of a decrepit old man, a grim reaper, or a ferryman, his visit is almost never welcome by the poor mortal who finds him at the door. Such is not the case in "Because I Could Not Stop for Death." Knowing that the woman has been keeping herself too busy in her daily life to remember Death, he "kindly" comes by to get her. Perhaps Dickinson's most famous work, "Because I Could Not Stop for Death" is generally considered to be one of the great masterpieces of American poetry. Here, Death is a gentleman, perhaps handsome and well-groomed, who makes a call at the home of a naïve young woman. The poem begins with a comment upon Death's politeness, although he surprises the woman with his visit. While most people would try to bar the door once they recognized his identity, this woman gives the impression that she is quite flattered to find herself in even this gentleman's favor. Death is personified, or described in terms of human characteristics, throughout literature. Figuratively speaking, this poem is about one woman's "date with death." Dickinson uses the personification of Death as a metaphor throughout the poem.

8. Which of the following sentence beginnings indicate the opening sentence of this paragraph?
   A. "Perhaps Dickinson's most..."
   B. "The poem begins with..."
   C. "Death is personified..."
   D. "Whether Death takes..."

   8.____

9. To whom does "his" refer to in the sentence that starts "While most people would..."?
   A. A gentleman
   B. Death
   C. People trying to avoid death
   D. Ms. Dickinson

   9.____

10. If the paragraph were correctly organized, the second to last sentence would end with:
    A. "...gentleman's favor."
    B. "...a naive young woman."
    C. "...of American poetry."
    D. "...throughout literature."

    10.____

Questions 11-13.

DIRECTIONS: Questions 11 through 13 are to be answered on the basis of the following paragraph.

Reformers such as Jacob Riis, author of *The Children of the Tenements* (1903), and George Creel, who with the assistance of Denver's juvenile court judge, Ben Lindsey, wrote *Children in Bondage* (1913), helped broaden awareness of the conditions under which many of the nation's poor children were reared. At the same time, changes were taking place in the way the childhood years were perceived. More and more Americans began to regard children as a national resource that deserved society's protection and guidance. In sharp contrast to these images of child workers worn down by the toil of their labor were the children of the middle class, who led quite different lives and whose progress was measured not in industrial output, but in ways increasingly seen as being vital to their development as productive citizens. Exhibitions of photographs of children employed in all sorts of economic pursuits, including those considered among the most dangerous and grueling, proved equally successful in pricking the public's conscience. When the United States was a nation of farms, shops, and small mills, the use of children to supplement a family's income was so common that it attracted little notice and even less concern. The nation's rapid and dramatic transformation into an industrialized society, however, changed the environment in which children labored and the conditions to which they were exposed.

11. When organized correctly, the third sentence in the above paragraph would start:
    A. "The nation's rapid..."
    B. "In sharp contrast..."
    C. "At the same time..."
    D. "Exhibitions of photographs..."

    11.____

12. If the author wanted to change the beginning of the topic sentence for this paragraph to "In the past," they would need to change which of the following?
    A. "Reformers such as..."
    B. "Exhibitions of photographs..."
    C. "More and more Americans..."
    D. "When the United States..."

    12.____

13. If the above paragraph was organized correctly, its ending words of the last sentence would be:

    13.____

A. "…as productive citizens."
B. "…and even less concern."
C. "…in pricking the public's conscience."
D. "…poor children were reared."

Questions 14-16.

DIRECTIONS: Questions 14 through 16 are to be answered on the basis of the following paragraph.

Here we outline a unique bivariate flood hazard assessment framework that accounts for the interactions between a primary oceanic flooding hazard, coastal water level, and fluvial flooding hazards. Common flood hazard assessment practices typically focus on one flood driver at a time and ignore potential compounding impacts. The results show that, in a warming climate, future sea level rise not only increases the failure probability, but also exacerbates the compounding effects of flood drivers. Using the notion of "failure probability," we also assess coastal flood hazard under different future sea level rise scenarios. Population and assets in coastal regions are threatened by both oceanic and fluvial flooding hazards.

14. When the sentences above are organized correctly, the paragraph starts with the sentence that begins:
    A. "The results show…"
    B. "Here we outline…"
    C. "Population and assets…"
    D. "Using the notion…"

14.____

15. If the author wanted to add the phrase "To sum up" to the above paragraph, he would insert it in front of the sentence that begins:
    A. "Using the notion…"
    B. "Common flood hazard…"
    C. "Here we outline…"
    D. "The results show…"

15.____

16. Assuming the paragraph were organized correctly, the second to last sentence would end:
    A. "…of flood drivers."
    B. "…level rise scenarios."
    C. "…fluvial flooding hazards."
    D. "…compounding impacts."

16.____

Questions 17-19.

DIRECTIONS: Questions 17 through 19 are to be answered on the basis of the following paragraph.

The adhesive stuck to a pig heart even when the surface was coated in blood, the team reported in the July 28 Science. Li, who did the research while at Harvard University, and colleagues also tested the glue in live rats with liver lacerations. A solution might be found under wet leaves on a forest floor, recent research suggests. For surgeons closing internal incisions, that's more than an annoyance. The right glue could hold wounds together as effectively as stitches and staples with less damage to the surrounding soft tissue, enabling safer surgical procedures. It stopped the rats' bleeding, and the animals didn't appear to suffer any bad reaction from the adhesive. Finding a great glue is a sticky task — especially if you want to attach to something as slick as the inside of the human body. Jianyu Li of McGill University in Montreal and colleagues have created a surgical glue that mimics the chemical recipe of goopy slime that slugs exude when they're startled. Using the glue to plug a hole in the pig heart worked so well that the heart still held in liquid after being inflated and deflated tens of thousands of times. Even the strongest human-made adhesives don't work well on wet surfaces like tissues and organs.

17. The above paragraph, when organized correctly, should begin with the words: 17._____
    A. "Finding a great..."   B. "Using the glue..."
    C. "The adhesive stuck..."   D. "It stopped the rats..."

18. If the author wanted to split the paragraph into two separate paragraphs, the 18._____
    first sentence of the second paragraph would begin:
    A. "For surgeons closing..."   B. "Even the strongest..."
    C. "A solution might be..."   D. "Jianyu Li of McGill..."

19. If the above paragraph were organized correctly, the final sentence would 19._____
    end with:
    A. "...recent research suggests."   B. "...from the adhesive."
    C. "...like tissues and organs."   D. "...thousands of times."

Questions 20-22.

DIRECTIONS: Questions 20 to 22 are to be answered on the basis of the following paragraph.

The signal from the spacecraft is gone, and within the next 45 seconds, so will be the spacecraft," Cassini project manager Earl Maize announced from the mission control center at NASA's Jet Propulsion Lab. The signal that Cassini had reached its destination arrived at Earth at 4:54 A.M., and cut out about a minute later as the spacecraft lost its battle with Saturn's atmosphere. I'm going to call this the end of mission. Project manager, off the net." With that, the mission control team erupted in applause, hugs and some tears. This has been an incredible mission, an incredible spacecraft, and you're all an incredible team. The spacecraft entered Saturn's atmosphere at about 3:31 A.M. PDT on September 15 and immediately began running through all of its stabilizing procedures to try to keep itself upright. Cassini went down fighting. After 20 years in space and 13 years orbiting Saturn, the veteran spacecraft spent its last 90 seconds or so firing its thrusters as hard as it could to keep sending Saturnian secrets back to Earth for as long as possible.

20. In the above paragraph, who does "you all" refer to in the sentence that begins 20._____
    "Congratulations"?
    A. All Americans   B. Cassini
    C. Earl Maize   D. The mission control team

21. If the sentence were organized correctly, the fourth sentence's last words 21._____
    would be:
    A. "...as long as possible."   B. "...this amazing accomplishment."
    C. "...Saturn's atmosphere."   D. "...off the net."

22. When organized correctly, the final sentence would end with the following: 22._____
    A. "...and some tears."   B. "...went down fighting."
    C. "...Jet Propulsion Lab."   D. "...keep itself upright."

Questions 23-25.

DIRECTIONS: Questions 23 through 25 are to be answered on the basis of the following paragraph.

As the first African-American woman to carry mail, she stood out on the trail — and became a Wild West legend. Born Mary Fields in around 1832, Fields was born into slavery, and like many other enslaved people, her exact date of birth is not known. Rumor had it that she'd fending off an angry pack of wolves with her rifle, had "the temperament of a grizzly bear," and was not above a gunfight. Bandits beware: In 1890s Montana, would-be mail thieves didn't stand a chance against Stagecoach Mary. Even the place of her birth is questionable, though historians have pinpointed Hickman County, Tennessee as the most likely location. At the time, slaves were treated like pieces of property; their numbers were recorded in record books, their names were not. But how much of Stagecoach Mary's story is myth? The hard-drinking, quick-shooting mail carrier sported two guns, men's clothing, and a bad attitude.

23. Who does "she'd" refer to in the sentence that begins "Rumor had it..."?
    A. An anonymous African-American
    B. Hickman County
    C. A mail thief
    D. Stagecoach Mary

24. If the author were interested in splitting this paragraph into two separate paragraphs, the topic sentence of the second paragraph would begin:
    A. "At the time…"
    B. "Born Mary Fields…"
    C. "Bandits beware…"
    D. "As the first…"

25. When organized correctly, the final sentence of the paragraph would end with the words:
    A. "…their names were not."
    B. "…above a gunfight."
    C. "…against Stagecoach Mary."
    D. "…a Wild West legend."

KEY (CORRECT ANSWERS)

1.	A	11.	C
2.	D	12.	D
3.	C	13.	A
4.	B	14.	C
5.	D	15.	D
6.	B	16.	B
7.	A	17.	A
8.	C	18.	C
9.	B	19.	B
10.	A	20.	D

21. C
22. A
23. D
24. B
25. A

TEST 2

DIRECTIONS: Each question or incomplete statement is followed by several suggested answers or completions. Select the one that BEST answers the question or completes the statement. *PRINT THE LETTER OF THE CORRECT ANSWER IN THE SPACE AT THE RIGHT.*

Questions 1-3.

DIRECTIONS: Questions 1 through 3 are to be answered on the basis of the following paragraph.

The majority of people who develop these issues are athletes who participate in popular high-impact sports, especially football. Although most people who suffer a concussion experience initial bouts of dizziness, nausea, and drowsiness, these symptoms often disappear after a few days. Although both new sports regulations and improvements in helmet technology can help protect players, the sports media and fans alike bear some of the responsibility for reducing the incidence of these devastating injuries. These psychological problems can include depression, anxiety, memory loss, inability to concentrate, and aggression. In extreme cases, people suffering from CTE have even committed suicide or homicide. The long-term effects of concussions, however, are less understood and far more severe. Recent studies suggest that people who suffer multiple concussions are at a significant risk for developing chronic traumatic encephalopathy (CTE), a degenerative brain disorder that causes a variety of dangerous mental and emotional problems to arise weeks, months, or even years after the initial injury. Chronic Traumatic Encephalopathy Concussions are brain injuries that occur when a person receives a blow to the head, face, or neck.

1. When organized correctly, the first sentence of the paragraph begins with: 1.____
   A. "Recent studies suggest…"   B. "The long-term effects…"
   C. "Although both new…"   D. "Chronic Traumatic…"

2. Upon ordering the paragraph correctly, the author wishes to substitute for a 2.____
   word in sentence four that means "progressive irreversible deterioration."
   Which word does the author wish to replace?
   A. Anxiety   B. Degenerative
   C. Responsibility   D. Devastating

3. If put in the right order, the paragraph's last words would be: 3.____
   A. "…to the head, face, or neck."
   B. "…committed suicide or homicide."
   C. "…these devastating injuries."
   D. "…far more severe."

2 (#2)

Questions 4-8.

DIRECTIONS: Questions 4 through 8 are to be answered on the basis of the following paragraph.

These controversies were settled by the 1977 treaty, which provided for a twenty-two-year period of U.S. withdrawal and turnover of the canal to Panama. For its first 85 years the canal was operate exclusively by the United States government as an international maritime passage, according to the 1903 Hay-Buneau-Varilla Treaty and the 1977 Carter-Torrijos Treaty that replaced it. Panamanian and other critics pointed out that the United States took unfair advantage of the newly independent republic (separated from Colombia in 1903, with the help of the United States) to impose conditions for near-sovereign ownership; complained that it exceeded its original concession by creating a strategic military complex with fourteen bases and numerous intelligence sites; and asserted that it created a virtual state within a state by establishing public agencies and enterprises in the 500-plus square miles of territory it controlled in the Canal Zone. One of the world's great engineering projects, the canal was controversial because of the method by which the United States gained the concession (by negotiating a treaty with a French shareholder temporarily representing Panama) and its operation of the utility with regard to the interests of Panama. Built between 1904 and 1914, the canal shortened maritime voyages considerably. The Panama Canal is a 51-mile ship canal with six pairs of locks that crosses the Isthmus of Panama and allows vessels to transit between the Caribbean Sea and the Pacific Ocean. Under the latter treaty, the canal was turned over in 1999 to the Republic of Panama, which has operated it ever since.

4. When organized correctly, the sentence AFTERs the topic sentence should begin:
   A. "Built between 1904..."
   B. "The Panama Canal..."
   C. "These controversies..."
   D. "Panamanian and other..."

4._____

5. If the author ordered the sentences correctly, one sentence that provides evidence of controversy surrounding the Panama Canal would be Sentence
   A. 7   B. 5   C. 1   D. 2

5._____

6. When correctly ordered, the last words of the paragraph would be:
   A. "...the canal to Panama."
   B. "...in the Canal Zone."
   C. "...and the Pacific Ocean."
   D. "...to the interests of Panama."

6._____

7. What "latter treaty" is the sentence that begins "Under the latter treaty..." referring to in the paragraph?
   A. The Treaty of Panama
   B. The Hay-Buneau-Varilla Treaty
   C. The Carter-Torrijos Treaty
   D. Both B and C

7._____

8. When organized correctly, the sentence that ends "...in the Canal Zone" would be preceded by the sentence that begins:
   A. "The Panama Canal..."
   B. "These controversies were..."
   C. "For its first..."
   D. "One of the world's great..."

8._____

Questions 9-11.

DIRECTIONS: Questions 9 through 11 are to be answered on the basis of the following paragraph.

Such incidents revolved around many issues, including, among others, job security, wages, occupational safety, and, especially, the eight-hour day. The Haymarket Riot of 1886 grew out of a long string of circumstances that eventually culminated in an unfortunate incident. Not only were skilled craftsmen seeing their professions disappear in the face of machines operated by unskilled labor, but the length of hours in the workday lengthened and could range from ten to twelve and even longer in some specific instances. It was this last issue that was particularly important as the Industrial Revolution truly swept over America. Regardless of who might have been at fault in a labor struggle, each moment of violent upheaval had serious consequences. During the post-Civil War era, there were periods of labor upheaval both in Chicago and across the nation. Each of these topics played an important role in labor unrest as the climate in the country between workers and the state reached fever pitch. At issue were several key points: the continued growth of the Industrial Revolution and its impact on society, the movement for the eight-hour workday, worker dissatisfaction, suppression of labor activities by various government authorities, and the growth of radicalism in the United States.

9. If the author were to put the paragraph in the correct order, the third sentence would begin with the words:
   A. "Each of these…"
   B. "It was this last…"
   C. "Not only were skilled…"
   D. "The Haymarket Riot…"

9.____

10. The author has determined that one paragraph is too long, so they wish to split it into two paragraphs and change the start of the new paragraph to "Dating back to". The sentence that the author would need to alter slightly currently begins:
    A. "The Haymarket Riot…"
    B. "Each of these topics…"
    C. "During the post-Civil…"
    D. "Not only were…"

10.____

11. When organized correctly, the last sentence of the paragraph would end with the words:
    A. "…an unfortunate incident."
    B. "…some specific instances."
    C. "…in the United States."
    D. "…across the nation."

11.____

Questions 12-14.

DIRECTIONS: Questions 12 through 14 are to be answered on the basis of the following paragraph.

Using an experimental design, they find no evidence that the use of Twitter improves students' learning. The authors assess students across three different institutions to see if the use of Twitter improves learning outcomes relative to a traditional Learning Management System. Ever since Becker and Watts (1996) found that economic educators rely heavily on "chalk and talk" as a primary teaching method, economic educators have been seeking new ways to engage students and improve learning outcomes. Recently, the use of social media as a pedagogical tool in economics has received increasing interest.

12. When organized correctly, the paragraph would begin with the words: 12.____
    A. "Using an..." B. "Recently, the..."
    C. "The authors..." D. "Ever since..."

13. In the sentence that begins "Using an experimental...", to whom does "they" refer? 13.____
    A. Social media users B. Becker and Watts
    C. Economic educators D. Different institutions

14. If the author wanted to start the last sentence with "With that said...", they would be adding it to the sentence that currently starts: 14.____
    A. "Using an..." B. "The authors..."
    C. "Recently, the..." D. "Ever since..."

Questions 15-17.

DIRECTIONS: Questions 15 through 17 are to be answered on the basis of the following paragraph.

Teaching the topic of genetics in relationship to ancestry and race generates many questions, and requires a teaching strategy that encourages perspective-based exploration and discussion. We have developed a set of dialogues for discussing the complex science of genetics, ancestry, and race that is contextualized in real human interactions and that contends with the social and ethical implications of this science. This article provides some brief historical and scientific context for these dialogues, describes their development, and relates how we have used them in different ways to engage diverse groups of science learners. The dialogue series can be incorporated into classroom or informal science education settings. After listening to or performing the dialogues and participating in a discussion, students will: (1) recognize misunderstandings about the relationship between DNA and race; (2) describe how DNA testing services assign geographic ancestry; (3) explain how scientific findings have been used historically to promote institutionalized racism and the role personal biases can play in science; (4) identify situations in their own life that have affected their understanding of genetics and race; and (5) discuss the potential consequences of the racialization of medicine as well as other fallacies about the connection of science and race.

15. If the author organized the above paragraph correctly, the fourth sentence would end with the words: 15.____
    A. "...connection of science and race."
    B. "...implications of this science."
    C. "...exploration and discussion."
    D. "...science education settings."

16. The author wishes to split the paragraph into two distinct paragraphs. When organized, the last sentence of the first paragraph would begin: 16.____
    A. "We have developed..." B. "This article proves..."
    C. "The dialogue series..." D. "Teaching the topic..."

17. When organized correctly, the last sentence would begin with the words: 17.____
    A. "After listening to…"   B. "Teaching the topic…"
    C. "We have developed…"   D. "This article provides…"

Questions 18-20.

DIRECTIONS: Questions 18 through 20 are to be answered on the basis of the following paragraph.

For example, Canadian Immigration officers have the power to deny persons with OWI convictions from crossing the border into Canada. Individuals who have been acquitted of an OWI can still be stopped at the border and denied entry. Some restrictions, however, are not known to individuals that have been charged with an OWI. In fact, if you have been arrested or convicted for driving under the influence of drugs or alcohol, regardless of whether it was a felony or a misdemeanor, you may be criminally inadmissible to Canada or denied entry. In order to receive an eTA, individuals have to disclose their criminal convictions, which may bar them from entering Canada. The restrictions imposed by an OWI conviction can be quite burdensome. Even if you will not be driving in Canada, you can still be denied entry. This stringent border patrol comes as a surprise to many U.S. citizens. Canadian Immigration Officials have introduced a new entry requirement, known as an Electronic Travel Authorization (eTA).

18. When organized correctly, the topic sentence of the paragraph would begin with   18.____
    the words:
    A. "This stringent border…"   B. "In fact, if…"
    C. "Canadian Immigration Officials…"   D. "The restrictions imposed…"

19. Once properly ordered, it would make the most sense to insert the words   19.____
    "With that being the case…" in front of the sentence that currently begins:
    A. "The restrictions imposed…"   B. "For example…"
    C. "Canadian Immigration Officials…"   D. "Even if you will…"

20. If the author were to put the paragraph in correct order, the second to last   20.____
    sentence would end with the words:
    A. "…border into Canada."   B. "…from entering Canada."
    C. "…to many U.S. citizens."   D. "…to Canada or denied entry."

Questions 21-25.

DIRECTIONS: Questions 21 through 25 are to be answered on the basis of the following paragraph.

Many instructors at the college level require that you use scholarly articles as sources when writing a research paper. Scholarly or peer-reviewed articles are written by experts in academic or professional fields. They are excellent sources for finding out what has been studied or researched on a topic as well as to find bibliographies that point to other relevant sources of information. Peer-reviewed journals require that articles are read and evaluated by experts in the field before they are accepted for publication. Although most scholarly articles are refereed or peer reviewed, some are not. Generally, instructors are happy with either peer-reviewed or scholarly articles, but if your article HAS to be peer-reviewed, you will need to find that information in the front of the journal, or use Ulrich's Periodicals Directory (Reference Z6941 U5) located behind the Reference Desk on the 2nd floor of the library. Look up your title and look for the Document Type: Journal, Academic/Scholarly. Articles that are peer-reviewed will have an arrow to the left of the title.

21. When organized correctly, the introductory sentence would begin with the words: 21.____
    - A. "They are excellent…"
    - B. "Peer-reviewed journals…"
    - C. "Many instructors at…"
    - D. "Look up your…"

22. In the sentence that begins "They are", to what/whom does "They" refer?   22.____
    - A. Scholarly articles
    - B. Instructors
    - C. Peers
    - D. Library directory

23. If the author were interested in splitting up the paragraph into two separate paragraphs, the topic sentence of the second paragraph would begin: 23.____
    - A. "Many instructors at…"
    - B. "Peer-reviewed journals…"
    - C. "Generally instructors are…"
    - D. "Scholarly or peer-reviewed…"

24. When organized correctly, the third sentence of the paragraph would end with the words: 24.____
    - A. "…a research paper."
    - B. "…of the title."
    - C. "…of the library."
    - D. "…sources of information."

25. If the author were to organize the paragraph correctly, the paragraph would end with the words: 25.____
    - A. "…some are not."
    - B. "…a research paper."
    - C. "…or professional fields."
    - D. "…of the title."

7 (#2)

KEY (CORRECT ANSWERS)

1.	D		11.	B
2.	B		12.	D
3.	C		13.	B
4.	A		14.	A
5.	B		15.	D
6.	A		16.	C
7.	C		17.	A
8.	D		18.	D
9.	A		19.	C
10.	C		20.	B

21. C
22. A
23. B
24. D
25. D

PHILOSOPHY, PRINCIPLES, PRACTICES, AND TECHNICS OF SUPERVISION, ADMINISTRATION, MANAGEMENT, AND ORGANIZATION

TABLE OF CONTENTS

	Page
MEANING OF SUPERVISION	1
THE OLD AND THE NEW SUPERVISION	1
THE EIGHT (8) BASIC PRINCIPLES OF THE NEW SUPERVISION	1
I. Principle of Responsibility	1
II. Principle of Authority	2
III. Principle of Self-Growth	2
IV. Principle of Individual Worth	2
V. Principle of Creative Leadership	2
VI. Principle of Success and Failure	2
VII. Principle of Science	3
VIII. Principle of Cooperation	3
WHAT IS ADMINISTRATION?	3
I. Practices Commonly Classed as "Supervisory"	3
II. Practices Commonly Classed as "Administrative"	3
III. Practices Commonly Classed as Both "Supervisory" and "Administrative"	4
RESPONSIBILITIES OF THE SUPERVISOR	4
COMPETENCIES OF THE SUPERVISOR	4
THE PROFESSIONAL SUPERVISOR-EMPLOYEE RELATIONSHIP	4
MINI-TEXT IN SUPERVISION, ADMINISTRATION, MANAGEMENT, AND ORGANIZATION	5
I. Brief Highlights	5
A. Levels of Management	6
B. What the Supervisor Must Learn	6
C. A Definition of Supervision	6
D. Elements of the Team Concept	6
E. Principles of Organization	6
F. The Four Important Parts of Every Job	7
G. Principles of Delegation	7
H. Principles of Effective Communications	7
I. Principles of Work Improvement	7
J. Areas of Job Improvement	7
K. Seven Key Points in Making Improvements	8

L.	Corrective Techniques for Job Improvement	8
M.	A Planning Checklist	8
N.	Five Characteristics of Good Directions	9
O.	Types of Directions	9
P.	Controls	9
Q.	Orienting the New Employee	9
R.	Checklist for Orienting New Employees	9
S.	Principles of Learning	10
T.	Causes of Poor Performance	10
U.	Four Major Steps in On-the-Job Instructions	10
V.	Employees Want Five Things	10
W.	Some Don'ts in Regard to Praise	11
X.	How to Gain Your Workers' Confidence	11
Y.	Sources of Employee Problems	11
Z.	The Supervisor's Key to Discipline	11
AA.	Five Important Processes of Management	12
BB.	When the Supervisor Fails to Plan	12
CC.	Fourteen General Principles of Management	12
DD.	Change	12

II. Brief Topical Summaries — 13

A.	Who/What is the Supervisor?	13
B.	The Sociology of Work	13
C.	Principles and Practices of Supervision	14
D.	Dynamic Leadership	14
E.	Processes for Solving Problems	15
F.	Training for Results	15
G.	Health, Safety, and Accident Prevention	16
H.	Equal Employment Opportunity	16
I.	Improving Communications	16
J.	Self-Development	17
K.	Teaching and Training	17
	1. The Teaching Process	17
	a. Preparation	17
	b. Presentation	18
	c. Summary	18
	d. Application	18
	e. Evaluation	18
	2. Teaching Methods	18
	a. Lecture	18
	b. Discussion	18
	c. Demonstration	19
	d. Performance	19
	e. Which Method to Use	19

PHILOSOPHY, PRINCIPLES, PRACTICES, AND TECHNICS
OF
SUPERVISION, ADMINISTRATION, MANAGEMENT, AND ORGANIZATION

MEANING OF SUPERVISION

The extension of the democratic philosophy has been accompanied by an extension in the scope of supervision. Modern leaders and supervisors no longer think of supervision in the narrow sense of being confined chiefly to visiting employees, supplying materials, or rating the staff. They regard supervision as being intimately related to all the concerned agencies of society, they speak of the supervisor's function in terms of "growth," rather than the "improvement" of employees.

This modern concept of supervision may be defined as follows: Supervision is leadership and the development of leadership within groups which are cooperatively engaged in inspection, research, training, guidance, and evaluation.

THE OLD AND THE NEW SUPERVISION

TRADITIONAL
1. Inspection
2. Focused on the employee
3. Visitation
4. Random and haphazard
5. Imposed and authoritarian
6. One person usually

MODERN
1. Study and analysis
2. Focused on aims, materials, methods, supervisors, employees, environment
3. Demonstrations, intervisitation, workshops, directed reading, bulletins, etc.
4. Definitely organized and planned (scientific)
5. Cooperative and democratic
6. Many persons involved (creative)

THE EIGHT (8) BASIC PRINCIPLES OF THE NEW SUPERVISION

I. Principle of Responsibility
   Authority to act and responsibility for acting must be joined.
   A. If you give responsibility, give authority.
   B. Define employee duties clearly.
   C. Protect employees from criticism by others.
   D. Recognize the rights as well as obligations of employees.
   E. Achieve the aims of a democratic society insofar as it is possible within the area of your work.
   F. Establish a situation favorable to training and learning.
   G. Accept ultimate responsibility for everything done in your section, unit, office, division, department.
   H. Good administration and good supervision are inseparable.

II. Principle of Authority
The success of the supervisor is measured by the extent to which the power of authority is not used.
   A. Exercise simplicity and informality in supervision
   B. Use the simplest machinery of supervision
   C. If it is good for the organization as a whole, it is probably justified.
   D. Seldom be arbitrary or authoritative.
   E. Do not base your work on the power of position or of personality.
   F. Permit and encourage the free expression of opinions.

III. Principle of Self-Growth
The success of the supervisor is measured by the extent to which, and the speed with which, he is no longer needed.
   A. Base criticism on principles, not on specifics.
   B. Point out higher activities to employees.
   C. Train for self-thinking by employees to meet new situations.
   D. Stimulate initiative, self-reliance, and individual responsibility
   E. Concentrate on stimulating the growth of employees rather than on removing defects.

IV. Principle of Individual Worth
Respect for the individual is a paramount consideration in supervision.
   A. Be human and sympathetic in dealing with employees.
   B. Don't nag about things to be done.
   C. Recognize the individual differences among employees and seek opportunities to permit best expression of each personality.

V. Principle of Creative Leadership
The best supervision is that which is not apparent to the employee.
   A. Stimulate, don't drive employees to creative action.
   B. Emphasize doing good things.
   C. Encourage employees to do what they do best.
   D. Do not be too greatly concerned with details of subject or method.
   E. Do not be concerned exclusively with immediate problems and activities.
   F. Reveal higher activities and make them both desired and maximally possible.
   G. Determine procedures in the light of each situation but see that these are derived from a sound basic philosophy.
   H. Aid, inspire, and lead so as to liberate the creative spirit latent in all good employees.

VI. Principle of Success and Failure
There are no unsuccessful employees, only unsuccessful supervisors who have failed to give proper leadership.
   A. Adapt suggestions to the capacities, attitudes, and prejudices of employees.
   B. Be gradual, be progressive, be persistent.
   C. Help the employee find the general principle; have the employee apply his own problem to the general principle.
   D. Give adequate appreciation for good work and honest effort.
   E. Anticipate employee difficulties and help to prevent them.
   F. Encourage employees to do the desirable things they will do anyway.
   G. Judge your supervision by the results it secures.

VII. Principle of Science
Successful supervision is scientific, objective, and experimental. It is based on facts, not on prejudices.
   A. Be cumulative in results.
   B. Never divorce your suggestions from the goals of training.
   C. Don't be impatient of results.
   D. Keep all matters on a professional, not a personal, level.
   E. Do not be concerned exclusively with immediate problems and activities.
   F. Use objective means of determining achievement and rating where possible.

VIII. Principle of Cooperation
Supervision is a cooperative enterprise between supervisor and employee.
   A. Begin with conditions as they are.
   B. Ask opinions of all involved when formulating policies.
   C. Organization is as good as its weakest link.
   D. Let employees help to determine policies and department programs.
   E. Be approachable and accessible—physically and mentally.
   F. Develop pleasant social relationships.

WHAT IS ADMINISTRATION

Administration is concerned with providing the environment, the material facilities, and the operational procedures that will promote the maximum growth and development of supervisors and employees. (Organization is an aspect and a concomitant of administration.)

There is no sharp line of demarcation between supervision and administration; these functions are intimately interrelated and, often, overlapping. They are complementary activities.

I. Practices Commonly Classed as "Supervisory"
   A. Conducting employees' conferences
   B. Visiting sections, units, offices, divisions, departments
   C. Arranging for demonstrations
   D. Examining plans
   E. Suggesting professional reading
   F. Interpreting bulletins
   G. Recommending in-service training courses
   H. Encouraging experimentation
   I. Appraising employee morale
   J. Providing for intervisitation

II. Practices Commonly Classified as "Administrative"
   A. Management of the office
   B. Arrangement of schedules for extra duties
   C. Assignment of rooms or areas
   D. Distribution of supplies
   E. Keeping records and reports
   F. Care of audio-visual materials
   G. Keeping inventory records
   H. Checking record cards and books

      I.   Programming special activities
      J.   Checking on the attendance and punctuality of employees

III.   Practices Commonly Classified as Both "Supervisory" and "Administrative"
      A.   Program construction
      B.   Testing or evaluating outcomes
      C.   Personnel accounting
      D.   Ordering instructional materials

RESPONSIBILITIES OF THE SUPERVISOR

A person employed in a supervisory capacity must constantly be able to improve his own efficiency and ability. He represent the employer to the employees and only continuous self-examination can make him a capable supervisor.

Leadership and training are the supervisor's responsibility. An efficient working unit is one in which the employees work with the supervisor. It is his job to bring out the best in his employees. He must always be relaxed, courteous, and calm in his association with his employees. Their feelings are important, and a harsh attitude does not develop the most efficient employees.

COMPETENCES OF THE SUPERVISOR

      I.   Complete knowledge of the duties and responsibilities of his position.
      II.   To be able to organize a job, plan ahead, and carry through.
      III.   To have self-confidence and initiative.
      IV.   To be able to handle the unexpected situation and make quick decisions.
      V.   To be able to properly train subordinates in the positions they are best suited for.
      VI.   To be able to keep good human relations among his subordinates.
      VII. To be able to keep good human relations between his subordinates and himself and to earn their respect and trust.

THE PROFESSIONAL SUPERVISOR-EMPLOYEE RELATIONSHIP

There are two kinds of efficiency: one kind is only apparent and is produced in organizations through the exercise of mere discipline; this is but a simulation of the second, or true, efficiency which springs from spontaneous cooperation. If you are a manager, no matter how great or small your responsibility, it is your job, in the final analysis, to create and develop this involuntary cooperation among the people whom you supervise. For, no matter how powerful a combination of money, machines, and materials a company may have, this is a dead and sterile thing without a team of willing, thinking, and articulate people to guide it.

The following 21 points are presented as indicative of the exemplary basic relationship that should exist between supervisor and employee:

1. Each person wants to be liked and respected by his fellow employee and wants to be treated with consideration and respect by his superior.
2. The most competent employee will make an error. However, in a unit where good relations exist between the supervisor and his employees, tenseness and fear do not exist. Thus, errors are not hidden or covered up, and the efficiency of a unit is not impaired.

3. Subordinates resent rules, regulations, or orders that are unreasonable or unexplained.
4. Subordinates are quick to resent unfairness, harshness, injustices, and favoritism.
5. An employee will accept responsibility if he knows that he will be complimented for a job well done, and not too harshly chastised for failure; that his supervisor will check the cause of the failure, and, if it was the supervisor's fault, he will assume the blame therefore. If it was the employee's fault, his supervisor will explain the correct method or means of handling the responsibility.
6. An employee wants to receive credit for a suggestion he has made, that is used. If a suggestion cannot be used, the employee is entitled to an explanation. The supervisor should not say "no" and close the subject.
7. Fear and worry slow up a worker's ability. Poor working environment can impair his physical and mental health. A good supervisor avoids forceful methods, threats, and arguments to get a job done.
8. A forceful supervisor is able to train his employees individually and as a team, and is able to motivate them in the proper channels.
9. A mature supervisor is able to properly evaluate his subordinates and to keep them happy and satisfied.
10. A sensitive supervisor will never patronize his subordinates.
11. A worthy supervisor will respect his employees' confidences.
12. Definite and clear-cut responsibilities should be assigned to each executive.
13. Responsibility should always be coupled with corresponding authority.
14. No change should be made in the scope or responsibilities of a position without a definite understanding to that effect on the part of all persons concerned.
15. No executive or employee, occupying a single position in the organization, should be subject to definite orders from more than one source.
16. Orders should never be given to subordinates over the head of a responsible executive. Rather than do this, the officer in question should be supplanted.
17. Criticisms of subordinates should, whoever possible, be made privately, and in no case should a subordinate be criticized in the presence of executives or employees of equal or lower rank.
18. No dispute or difference between executives or employees as to authority or responsibilities should be considered too trivial for prompt and careful adjudication.
19. Promotions, wage changes, and disciplinary action should always be approved by the executive immediately superior to the one directly responsible.
20. No executive or employee should ever be required, or expected, to be at the same time an assistant to, and critic of, another.
21. Any executive whose work is subject to regular inspection should, wherever practicable, be given the assistance and facilities necessary to enable him to maintain an independent check of the quality of his work.

MINI-TEXT IN SUPERVISION, ADMINISTRATION, MANAGEMENT, AND ORGANIZATION

I. Brief Highlights

Listed concisely and sequentially are major headings and important data in the field for quick recall and review.

A. Levels of Management
Any organization of some size has several levels of management. In terms of a ladder, the levels are:

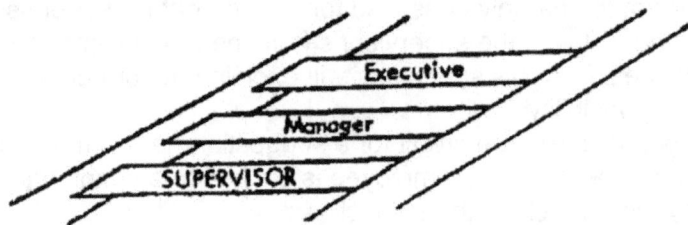

The first level is very important because it is the beginning point of management leadership.

B. What the Supervisor Must Learn
A supervisor must learn to:
1. Deal with people and their differences
2. Get the job done through people
3. Recognize the problems when they exist
4. Overcome obstacles to good performance
5. Evaluate the performance of people
6. Check his own performance in terms of accomplishment

C. A Definition of Supervisor
The term supervisor means any individual having authority, in the interests of the employer, to hire, transfer, suspend, lay-off, recall, promote, discharge, assign, reward, or discipline other employees or responsibility to direct them, or to adjust their grievances, or effectively to recommend such action, if, in connection with the foregoing, exercise of such authority is not of a merely routine or clerical nature but requires the use of independent judgment.

D. Elements of the Team Concept
What is involved in teamwork? The component parts are:
1. Members
2. A leader
3. Goals
4. Plans
5. Cooperation
6. Spirit

E. Principles of Organization
1. A team member must know what his job is.
2. Be sure that the nature and scope of a job are understood.
3. Authority and responsibility should be carefully spelled out.
4. A supervisor should be permitted to make the maximum number of decisions affecting his employees.
5. Employees should report to only one supervisor.
6. A supervisor should direct only as many employees as he can handle effectively.
7. An organization plan should be flexible.

8. Inspection and performance of work should be separate.
9. Organizational problems should receive immediate attention.
10. Assign work in line with ability and experience.

F. The Four Important Parts of Every Job
1. Inherent in every job is the *accountability* for results.
2. A second set of factors in every job is *responsibilities*.
3. Along with duties and responsibilities one must have the *authority* to act within certain limits without obtaining permission to proceed.
4. No job exists in a vacuum. The supervisor is surrounded by key *relationships*.

G. Principles of Delegation
Where work is delegated for the first time, the supervisor should think in terms of these questions:
1. Who is best qualified to do this?
2. Can an employee improve his abilities by doing this?
3. How long should an employee spend on this?
4. Are there any special problems for which he will need guidance?
5. How broad a delegation can I make?

H. Principles of Effective Communications
1. Determine the media.
2. To whom directed?
3. Identification and source authority.
4. Is communication understood?

I. Principles of Work Improvement
1. Most people usually do only the work which is assigned to them.
2. Workers are likely to fit assigned work into the time available to perform it.
3. A good workload usually stimulates output.
4. People usually do their best work when they know that results will be reviewed or inspected.
5. Employees usually feel that someone else is responsible for conditions of work, workplace layout, job methods, type of tools/equipment, and other such factors.
6. Employees are usually defensive about their job security.
7. Employees have natural resistance to change.
8. Employees can support or destroy a supervisor.
9. A supervisor usually earns the respect of his people through his personal example of diligence and efficiency.

J. Areas of Job Improvement
The areas of job improvement are quite numerous, but the most common ones which a supervisor can identify and utilize are:
1. Departmental layout
2. Flow of work
3. Workplace layout
4. Utilization of manpower
5. Work methods
6. Materials handling

7. Utilization
8. Motion economy

K. Seven Key Points in Making Improvements
1. Select the job to be improved
2. Study how it is being done now
3. Question the present method
4. Determine actions to be taken
5. Chart proposed method
6. Get approval and apply
7. Solicit worker participation

l. Corrective Techniques of Job Improvement
Specific Problems
1. Size of workload
2. Inability to meet schedules
3. Strain and fatigue
4. Improper use of men and skills
5. Waste, poor quality, unsafe conditions
6. Bottleneck conditions that hinder output
7. Poor utilization of equipment and machine
8. Efficiency and productivity of labor

General Improvement
1. Departmental layout
2. Flow of work
3. Work plan layout
4. Utilization of manpower
5. Work methods
6. Materials handling
7. Utilization of equipment
8. Motion economy

Corrective Techniques
1. Study with scale model
2. Flow chart study
3. Motion analysis
4. Comparison of units produced to standard allowance
5. Methods analysis
6. Flow chart and equipment study
7. Down time vs. running time
8. Motion analysis

M. A Planning Checklist
1. Objectives
2. Controls
3. Delegations
4. Communications
5. Resources
6. Manpower

7. Equipment
8. Supplies and materials
9. Utilization of time
10. Safety
11. Money
12. Work
13. Timing of improvements

N. Five Characteristics of Good Directions
In order to get results, directions must be:
1. Possible of accomplishment
2. Agreeable with worker interests
3. Related to mission
4. Planned and complete
5. Unmistakably clear

O. Types of Directions
1. Demands or direct orders
2. Requests
3. Suggestion or implication
4. volunteering

P. Controls
A typical listing of the overall areas in which the supervisor should establish controls might be:
1. Manpower
2. Materials
3. Quality of work
4. Quantity of work
5. Time
6. Space
7. Money
8. Methods

Q. Orienting the New Employee
1. Prepare for him
2. Welcome the new employee
3. Orientation for the job
4. Follow-up

R. Checklist for Orienting New Employees   Yes   No
1. Do you appreciate the feelings of new employees
   when they first report for work?   ___   ___
2. Are you aware of the fact that the new employee must
   make a big adjustment to his job?   ___   ___
3. Have you given him good reasons for liking the job and
   the organization?   ___   ___
4. Have you prepared for his first day on the job?   ___   ___
5. Did you welcome him cordially and make him feel needed?   ___   ___

	Yes	No

6. Did you establish rapport with him so that he feels free to talk and discuss matters with you? ___ ___
7. Did you explain his job to him and his relationship to you? ___ ___
8. Does he know that his work will be evaluated periodically on a basis that is fair and objective? ___ ___
9. Did you introduce him to his fellow workers in such a way that they are likely to accept him? ___ ___
10. Does he know what employee benefits he will receive? ___ ___
11. Does he understand the importance of being on the job and what to do if he must leave his duty station? ___ ___
12. Has he been impressed with the importance of accident prevention and safe practice? ___ ___
13. Does he generally know his way around the department? ___ ___
14. Is he under the guidance of a sponsor who will teach the right way of doing things? ___ ___
15. Do you plan to follow-up so that he will continue to adjust successfully to his job? ___ ___

S. Principles of Learning
   1. Motivation
   2. Demonstration or explanation
   3. Practice

T. Causes of Poor Performance
   1. Improper training for job
   2. Wrong tools
   3. Inadequate directions
   4. Lack of supervisory follow-up
   5. Poor communications
   6. Lack of standards of performance
   7. Wrong work habits
   8. Low morale
   9. Other

U. Four Major Steps in On-The-Job Instruction
   1. Prepare the worker
   2. Present the operation
   3. Tryout performance
   4. Follow-up

V. Employees Want Five Things
   1. Security
   2. Opportunity
   3. Recognition
   4. Inclusion
   5. Expression

W. Some Don'ts in Regard to Praise
   1. Don't praise a person for something he hasn't done.
   2. Don't praise a person unless you can be sincere.
   3. Don't be sparing in praise just because your superior withholds it from you.
   4. Don't let too much time elapse between good performance and recognition of it

X. How to Gain Your Workers' Confidence
   Methods of developing confidence include such things as:
   1. Knowing the interests, habits, hobbies of employees
   2. Admitting your own inadequacies
   3. Sharing and telling of confidence in others
   4. Supporting people when they are in trouble
   5. Delegating matters that can be well handled
   6. Being frank and straightforward about problems and working conditions
   7. Encouraging others to bring their problems to you
   8. Taking action on problems which impede worker progress

Y. Sources of Employee Problems
   On-the-job causes might be such things as:
   1. A feeling that favoritism is exercised in assignments
   2. Assignment of overtime
   3. An undue amount of supervision
   4. Changing methods or systems
   5. Stealing of ideas or trade secrets
   6. Lack of interest in job
   7. Threat of reduction in force
   8. Ignorance or lack of communications
   9. Poor equipment
   10. Lack of knowing how supervisor feels toward employee
   11. Shift assignments

   Off-the-job problems might have to do with:
   1. Health
   2. Finances
   3. Housing
   4. Family

Z. The Supervisor's Key to Discipline
   There are several key points about discipline which the supervisor should keep in mind:
   1. Job discipline is one of the disciplines of life and is directed by the supervisor.
   2. It is more important to correct an employee fault than to fix blame for it.
   3. Employee performance is affected by problems both on the job and off.
   4. Sudden or abrupt changes in behavior can be indications of important employee problems.
   5. Problems should be dealt with as soon as possible after they are identified.
   6. The attitude of the supervisor may have more to do with solving problems than the techniques of problem solving.
   7. Correction of employee behavior should be resorted to only after the supervisor is sure that training or counseling will not be helpful.

8. Be sure to document your disciplinary actions.
9. Make sure that you are disciplining on the basis of facts rather than personal feelings.
10. Take each disciplinary step in order, being careful not to make snap judgments, or decisions based on impatience.

AA. Five Important Processes of Management
1. Planning
2. Organizing
3. Scheduling
4. Controlling
5. Motivating

BB. When the Supervisor Fails to Plan
1. Supervisor creates impression of not knowing his job
2. May lead to excessive overtime
3. Job runs itself—supervisor lacks control
4. Deadlines and appointments missed
5. Parts of the work go undone
6. Work interrupted by emergencies
7. Sets a bad example
8. Uneven workload creates peaks and valleys
9. Too much time on minor details at expense of more important tasks

CC. Fourteen General Principles of Management
1. Division of work
2. Authority and responsibility
3. Discipline
4. Unity of command
5. Unity of direction
6. Subordination of individual interest to general interest
7. Remuneration of personnel
8. Centralization
9. Scalar chain
10. Order
11. Equity
12. Stability of tenure of personnel
13. Initiative
14. Esprit de corps

DD. Change

Bringing about change is perhaps attempted more often, and yet less well understood, than anything else the supervisor does. How do people generally react to change? (People tend to resist change that is imposed upon them by other individuals or circumstances.

Change is characteristic of every situation. It is a part of every real endeavor where the efforts of people are concerned.

1. Why do people resist change?
   People may resist change because of:
   a. Fear of the unknown
   b. Implied criticism
   c. Unpleasant experiences in the past
   d. Fear of loss of status
   e. Threat to the ego
   f. Fear of loss of economic stability

2. How can we best overcome the resistance to change?
   In initiating change, take these steps:
   a. Get ready to sell
   b. Identify sources of help
   c. Anticipate objections
   d. Sell benefits
   e. Listen in depth
   f. Follow up

II. Brief Topical Summaries

   A. Who/What is the Supervisor?
      1. The supervisor is often called the "highest level employee and the lowest level manager."
      2. A supervisor is a member of both management and the work group. He acts as a bridge between the two.
      3. Most problems in supervision are in the area of human relations, or people problems.
      4. Employees expect: Respect, opportunity to learn and to advance, and a sense of belonging, and so forth.
      5. Supervisors are responsible for directing people and organizing work. Planning is of paramount importance.
      6. A position description is a set of duties and responsibilities inherent to a given position.
      7. It is important to keep the position description up-to-date and to provide each employee with his own copy.

   B. The Sociology of Work
      1. People are alike in many ways; however, each individual is unique.
      2. The supervisor is challenged in getting to know employee differences. Acquiring skills in evaluating individuals is an asset.
      3. Maintaining meaningful working relationships in the organization is of great importance.
      4. The supervisor has an obligation to help individuals to develop to their fullest potential.
      5. Job rotation on a planned basis helps to build versatility and to maintain interest and enthusiasm in work groups.
      6. Cross training (job rotation) provides backup skills.

7. The supervisor can help reduce tension by maintaining a sense of humor, providing guidance to employees, and by making reasonable and timely decisions. Employees respond favorably to working under reasonably predictable circumstances.
8. Change is characteristic of all managerial behavior. The supervisor must adjust to changes in procedures, new methods, technological changes, and to a number of new and sometimes challenging situations.
9. To overcome the natural tendency for people to resist change, the supervisor should become more skillful in initiating change.

C. Principles and Practices of Supervision
1. Employees should be required to answer to only one superior.
2. A supervisor can effectively direct only a limited number of employees, depending upon the complexity, variety, and proximity of the jobs involved.
3. The organizational chart presents the organization in graphic form. It reflects lines of authority and responsibility as well as interrelationships of units within the organization.
4. Distribution of work can be improved through an analysis using the "Work Distribution Chart."
5. The "Work Distribution Chart" reflects the division of work within a unit in understandable form.
6. When related tasks are given to an employee, he has a better chance of increasing his skills through training.
7. The individual who is given the responsibility for tasks must also be given the appropriate authority to insure adequate results.
8. The supervisor should delegate repetitive, routine work. Preparation of recurring reports, maintaining leave and attendance records are some examples.
9. Good discipline is essential to good task performance. Discipline is reflected in the actions of employees on the job in the absence of supervision.
10. Disciplinary action may have to be taken when the positive aspects of discipline have failed. Reprimand, warning, and suspension are examples of disciplinary action.
11. If a situation calls for a reprimand, be sure it is deserved and remember it is to be done in private.

D. Dynamic Leadership
1. A style is a personal method or manner of exerting influence.
2. Authoritarian leaders often see themselves as the source of power and authority.
3. The democratic leader often perceives the group as the source of authority and power.
4. Supervisors tend to do better when using the pattern of leadership that is most natural for them.
5. Social scientists suggest that the effective supervisor use the leadership style that best fits the problem or circumstances involved.
6. All four styles—telling, selling, consulting, joining—have their place. Using one does not preclude using the other at another time.

7. The theory X point of view assumes that the average person dislikes work, will avoid it whenever possible, and must be coerced to achieve organizational objectives.
8. The theory Y point of view assumes that the average person considers work to be a natural as play, and, when the individual is committed, he requires little supervision or direction to accomplish desired objectives.
9. The leader's basic assumptions concerning human behavior and human nature affect his actions, decisions, and other managerial practices.
10. Dissatisfaction among employees is often present, but difficult to isolate. The supervisor should seek to weaken dissatisfaction by keeping promises, being sincere and considerate, keeping employees informed, and so forth.
11. Constructive suggestions should be encouraged during the natural progress of the work.

E. Processes for Solving Problems
1. People find their daily tasks more meaningful and satisfying when they can improve them.
2. The causes of problems, or the key factors, are often hidden in the background. Ability to solve problems often involves the ability to isolate them from their backgrounds. There is some substance to the cliché that some persons "can't see the forest for the trees."
3. New procedures are often developed from old ones. Problems should be broken down into manageable parts. New ideas can be adapted from old one.
4. People think differently in problem-solving situations. Using a logical, patterned approach is often useful. One approach found to be useful includes these steps:
   a. Define the problem
   b. Establish objectives
   c. Get the facts
   d. Weigh and decide
   e. Take action
   f. Evaluate action

F. Training for Results
1. Participants respond best when they feel training is important to them.
2. The supervisor has responsibility for the training and development of those who report to him.
3. When training is delegated to others, great care must be exercised to insure the trainer has knowledge, aptitude, and interest for his work as a trainer.
4. Training (learning) of some type goes on continually. The most successful supervisor makes certain the learning contributes in a productive manner to operational goals.
5. New employees are particularly susceptible to training. Older employees facing new job situations require specific training, as well as having need for development and growth opportunities.
6. Training needs require continuous monitoring.
7. The training officer of an agency is a professional with a responsibility to assist supervisors in solving training problems.

8. Many of the self-development steps important to the supervisor's own growth are equally important to the development of peers and subordinates. Knowledge of these is important when the supervisor consults with others on development and growth opportunities.

G. Health, Safety, and Accident Prevention
1. Management-minded supervisors take appropriate measures to assist employees in maintaining health and in assuring safe practices in the work environment.
2. Effective safety training and practices help to avoid injury and accidents.
3. Safety should be a management goal. All infractions of safety which are observed should be corrected without exception.
4. Employees' safety attitude, training and instruction, provision of safe tools and equipment, supervision, and leadership are considered highly important factors which contribute to safety and which can be influenced directly by supervisors.
5. When accidents do occur, they should be investigated promptly for very important reasons, including the fact that information which is gained can be used to prevent accidents in the future.

H. Equal Employment Opportunity
1. The supervisor should endeavor to treat all employees fairly, without regard to religion, race, sex, or national origin.
2. Groups tend to reflect the attitude of the leader. Prejudice can be detected even in very subtle form. Supervisors must strive to create a feeling of mutual respect and confidence in every employee.
3. Complete utilization of all human resources is a national goal. Equitable consideration should be accorded women in the work force, minority-group members, the physically and mentally handicapped, and the older employee. The important question is: "Who can do the job?"
4. Training opportunities, recognition for performance, overtime assignments, promotional opportunities, and all other personnel actions are to be handled on an equitable basis.

I. Improving Communications
1. Communications is achieving understanding between the sender and the receiver of a message. It also means sharing information—the creation of understanding.
2. Communication is basic to all human activity. Words are means of conveying meanings; however, real meanings are in people.
3. There are very practical differences in the effectiveness of one-way, impersonal, and two-way communications. Words spoken face-to-face are better understood. Telephone conversations are effective, but lack the rapport of person-to-person exchanges. The whole person communicates.
4. Cooperation and communication in an organization go hand in hand. When there is a mutual respect between people, spelling out rules and procedures for communicating is unnecessary.
5. There are several barriers to effective communications. These include failure to listen with respect and understanding, lack of skill in feedback, and misinterpreting the meanings of words used by the speaker. It is also common

practice to listen to what we want to hear, and tune out things we do not want to hear.
6. Communication is management's chief problem. The supervisor should accept the challenge to communicate more effectively and to improve interagency and intra-agency communications.
7. The supervisor may often plan for and conduct meetings. The planning phase is critical and may determine the success or the failure of a meeting.
8. Speaking before groups usually requires extra effort. Stage fright may never disappear completely, but it can be controlled.

J. Self-Development
1. Every employee is responsible for his own self-development.
2. Toastmaster and toastmistress clubs offer opportunities to improve skills in oral communications.
3. Planning for one's own self-development is of vital importance. Supervisors know their own strengths and limitations better than anyone else.
4. Many opportunities are open to aid the supervisor in his developmental efforts, including job assignments; training opportunities, both governmental and non-governmental—to include universities and professional conferences and seminars.
5. Programmed instruction offers a means of studying at one's own rate.
6. Where difficulties may arise from a supervisor's being away from his work for training, he may participate in televised home study or correspondence courses to meet his self-development needs.

K. Teaching and Training
1. The Teaching Process
Teaching is encouraging and guiding the learning activities of students toward established goals. In most cases this process consists of five steps: preparation, presentation, summarization, evaluation, and application.

   a. Preparation
   Preparation is two-fold in nature; that of the supervisor and the employee. Preparation by the supervisor is absolutely essential to success. He must know what, when, where, how, and whom he will teach. Some of the factors that should be considered are:
   1) The objectives
   2) The materials needed
   3) The methods to be used
   4) Employee participation
   5) Employee interest
   6) Training aids
   7) Evaluation
   8) Summarization

   Employee preparation consists in preparing the employee to receive the material. Probably the most important single factor in the preparation of the employee is arousing and maintaining his interest. He must know the objectives of the training, why he is there, how the material can be used, and its importance to him.

b. Presentation
In presentation, have a carefully designed plan and follow it. The plan should be accurate and complete, yet flexible enough to meet situations as they arise. The method of presentation will be determined by the particular situation and objectives.

c. Summary
A summary should be made at the end of every training unit and program. In addition, there may be internal summaries depending on the nature of the material being taught. The important thing is that the trainee must always be able to understand how each part of the new material relates to the whole.

d. Application
The supervisor must arrange work so the employee will be given a chance to apply new knowledge or skills while the material is still clear in his mind and interest is high. The trainee does not really know whether he has learned the material until he has been given a chance to apply it. If the material is not applied, it loses most of its value.

e. Evaluation
The purpose of all training is to promote learning. To determine whether the training has been a success or failure, the supervisor must evaluate this learning.
In the broadest sense, evaluation includes all the devices, methods, skills, and techniques used by the supervisor to keep himself and the employees informed as to their progress toward the objectives they are pursuing. The extent to which the employee has mastered the knowledge, skills, and abilities, or changed his attitudes, as determined by the program objectives, is the extent to which instruction has succeeded or failed.
Evaluation should not be confined to the end of the lesson, day, or program but should be used continuously. We shall note later the way this relates to the rest of the teaching process.

2. Teaching Methods
A teaching method is a pattern of identifiable student and instructor activity used in presenting training material.
All supervisors are faced with the problem of deciding which method should be used at a given time.

a. Lecture
The lecture is direct oral presentation of material by the supervisor. The present trend is to place less emphasis on the trainer's activity and more on that of the trainee.

b. Discussion
Teaching by discussion or conference involves using questions and other techniques to arouse interest and focus attention upon certain areas, and by doing so creating a learning situation. This can be one of the most

valuable methods because it gives the employees an opportunity to express their ideas and pool their knowledge.

    c. Demonstration
The demonstration is used to teach how something works or how to do something. It can be used to show a principle or what the results of a series of actions will be. A well-staged demonstration is particularly effective because it shows proper methods of performance in a realistic manner.

    d. Performance
Performance is one of the most fundamental of all learning techniques or teaching methods. The trainee may be able to tell how a specific operation should be performed but he cannot be sure he knows how to perform the operation until he has done so.
As with all methods, there are certain advantages and disadvantages to each method.

    e. Which Method to Use
Moreover, there are other methods and techniques of teaching. It is difficult to use any method without other methods entering into it. In any learning situation, a combination of methods is usually more effective than any one method alone.

Finally, evaluation must be integrated into the other aspects of the teaching-learning process.

It must be used in the motivation of the trainees; it must be used to assist in developing understanding during the training; and it must be related to employee application of the results of training.

This is distinctly the role of the supervisor.

GLOSSARY OF PROJECT MANAGEMENT

A

Agile software development is a set of fundamental principles about how software should be developed based on an agile way of working in contrast to previous heavy-handed software development methodologies.

Aggregate planning is an operational activity which does an aggregate plan for the production process, in advance of 2 to 18 months, to give an idea to management as to what quantity of materials and other resources are to be procured and when, so that the total cost of operations of the organization is kept to the minimum over that period.

Allocation is the assignment of available resources in an economic way.

B

Budget generally refers to a list of all planned expenses and revenues.

Budgeted cost of work performed (BCWP) measures the budgeted cost of work that has actually been performed, rather than the cost of work scheduled.

Budgeted cost of work scheduled (BCWS) the approved budget that has been allocated to complete a scheduled task (or Work Breakdown Structure (WBS) component) during a specific time period.

Business model is a profit-producing system that has an important degree of independence from the other systems within an enterprise.

Business analysis is the set of tasks, knowledge, and techniques required to identify business needs and determine solutions to business problems. Solutions often include a systems development component, but may also consist of process improvement or organizational change.

Business operations are those ongoing recurring activities involved in the running of a business for the purpose of producing value for the stakeholders. They are contrasted with project management, and consist of business processes.

Business process is a collection of related, structured activities or tasks that produce a specific service or product (serve a particular goal) for a particular customer or customers. There are three types of business processes: Management processes, Operational processes, and Supporting processes.

Business Process Modeling (BPM) is the activity of representing processes of an enterprise, so that the current ("as is") process may be analyzed and improved in future ("to be").

C

Capability Maturity Model.

Capability Maturity Model (CMM) in software engineering is a model of the maturity of the capability of certain business processes. A maturity model can be described as a structured collection of elements that describe certain aspects of maturity in an organization, and aids in the definition and understanding of an organization's processes.

Change control is the procedures used to ensure that changes (normally, but not necessarily, to IT systems) are introduced in a controlled and coordinated manner. Change control is a major aspect of the broader discipline of change management.

Change management is a field of management focused on organizational changes. It aims to ensure that methods and procedures are used for efficient and prompt handling of all changes to controlled IT infrastructure, in order to minimize the number and impact of any related incidents upon service.

Case study is a research method which involves an in-depth, longitudinal examination of a single instance or event: a case. They provide a systematic way of looking at events, collecting data, analyzing information, and reporting the results.

Certified Associate in Project Management is an entry-level certification for project practitioners offered by Project Management Institute.

Communications Log is an on-going documentation of communication events between any identified project stakeholders, managed and collected by the project manager that describes: the sender and receiver of the communication event; where, when and for how long the communication event elapsed; in what form the communication event took place; a summary of what information was communicated; what actions/outcomes should be taken as a result of the communication event; and to what level of priority should the actions/outcomes of the communication event be graded

Constructability is a project management technique to review the construction processes from start to finish during pre-construction phrase. It will identify obstacles before a project is actually built to reduce or prevent error, delays, and cost overrun.

Costs in economics, business, and accounting are the value of money that has been used up to produce something, and hence is not available for use anymore. In business, the cost may be one of acquisition, in which case the amount of money expended to acquire it is counted as cost.

Cost engineering is the area of engineering practice where engineering judgment and experience are used in the application of scientific principles and techniques to problems of cost estimating, cost control, business planning and management science, profitability analysis, project management, and planning and scheduling."[

Construction, in the fields of architecture and civil engineering, is a process that consists of the building or assembling of infrastructure. Far from being a single activity, large scale construction is a feat of multitasking. Normally the job is managed by the project manager and supervised by the construction manager, design engineer, construction engineer or project architect.

Cost overrun is defined as excess of actual cost over budget.

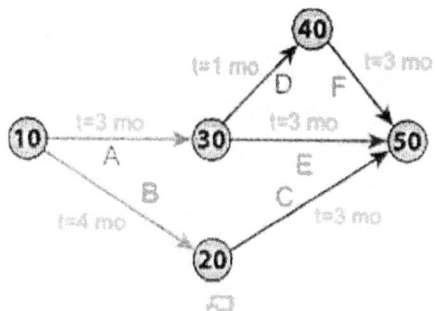

PERT chart with two critical paths.

Critical path method (CPM) is a mathematically based modeling technique for scheduling a set of project activities, used in project management.

Critical chain project management (CCPM) is a method of planning and managing projects that puts more emphasis on the resources required to execute project tasks.

D

Dependency in a project network is a link amongst a project's terminal elements.

Dynamic Systems Development Method (DSDM) is a software development methodology originally based upon the Rapid Application Development methodology. DSDM is an iterative and incremental approach that emphasizes continuous user involvement.

Duration of a project's terminal element is the number of calendar periods it takes from the time the execution of element starts to the moment it is completed.

Deliverable A contractually required work product, produced and delivered to a required state. A deliverable may be a document, hardware, software or other tangible product.

E

Earned schedule (ES) is an extension to earned value management (EVM), which renames two traditional measures, to indicate clearly they are in units of currency or quantity, not time.

Earned value management (EVM) is a project management technique for measuring project progress in an objective manner, with a combination of measuring scope, schedule, and cost in a single integrated system.

Effort management is a project management subdiscipline for effective and efficient use of time and resources to perform activities regarding quantity, quality and direction.

Enterprise modeling is the process of understanding an enterprise business and improving its performance through creation of enterprise models. This includes the modelling of the relevant business domain (usually relatively stable), business processes (usually more volatile), and Information technology

Estimation in project management is the processes of making accurate estimates using the appropriate techniques.

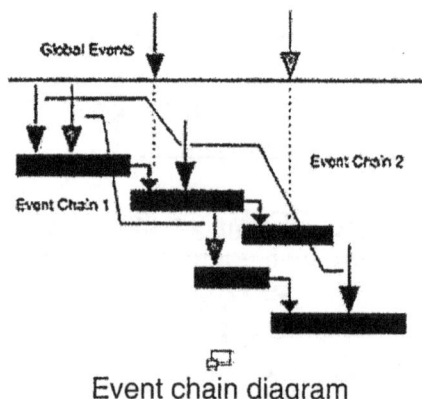

Event chain diagram

Event chain diagram : diagram that show the relationships between events and tasks and how the events affect each other.

Event chain methodology is an uncertainty modeling and schedule network analysis technique that is focused on identifying and managing events and event chains that affect project schedules.

Extreme project management (XPM) refers to a method of managing very complex and very uncertain projects.

F

Float in a project network is the amount of time that a task in a project network can be delayed without causing a delay to subsequent tasks and or the project completion date.

Focused Improvement in Theory of Constraints is the ensemble of activities aimed at elevating the performance of any system, especially a business system, with respect to its goal by eliminating its constraints one by one and by not working on non-constraints.

Fordism, named after Henry Ford, refers to various social theories. It has varying but related meanings in different fields, and for Marxist and non-Marxist scholars.

G

Henry Gantt was an American mechanical engineer and management consultant, who developed the Gantt chart in the 1910s.

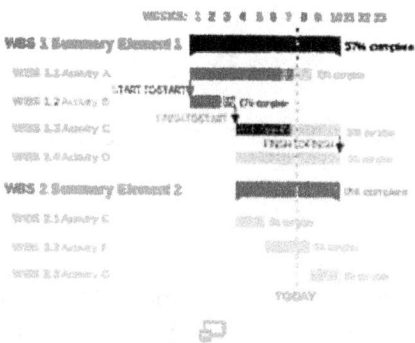

A Gantt chart.

Gantt chart is a type of bar chart that illustrates a project schedule. It illustrate the start and finish dates of the terminal elements and summary elements of a project. Terminal elements and summary elements comprise the work breakdown structure of the project.

Goal or objective consists of a projected state of affairs which a person or a system plans or intends to achieve or bring about — a personal or organizational desired end-point in some sort of assumed development. Many people endeavor to reach goals within a finite time by setting deadlines

Goal setting involves establishing specific, measurable and time targeted objectives

Graphical Evaluation and Review Technique (GERT) is a network analysis technique that allows probabilistic treatment of both network logic and activity duration estimated.

H

Hammock activity is a grouping of subtasks that "hangs" between two end dates it is tied to (or the two end-events it is fixed to).

HERMES is a Project Management Method developed by the Swiss Government, based on the German V-Modell. The first domain of application was software projects.

I

Integrated Master Plan (IMP) is an event-based, top level plan, consisting of a hierarchy of Program Events.

ISO 10006 is a guidelines for quality management in projects, is an international standard developed by the International Organization for Standardization.

Iterative and Incremental development is a cyclic software development process developed in response to the weaknesses of the waterfall model. It starts with an initial planning and ends with deployment with the cyclic interaction in between

K

Kickoff meeting is the first meeting with the project team and the client of the project.

L

Level of Effort (LOE) is qualified as a support type activity which doesn't lend itself to measurement of a discrete accomplishment. Examples of such an activity may be project budget accounting, customer liaison, etc.

Linear scheduling method (LSM) is a graphical scheduling method focusing on continuous resource utilization in repetitive activities. It is believed that it originally adopted the idea of Line-Of-Balance method.

Lean manufacturing or lean production, which is often known simply as "Lean", is the practice of a theory of production that considers the expenditure of resources for any means other than the creation of value for the presumed customer to be wasteful, and thus a target for elimination.

M

Management in business and human organization activity is simply the act of getting people together to accomplish desired goals. Management comprises planning, organizing, staffing, leading or directing, and controlling an organization (a group of one or more people or entities) or effort for the purpose of accomplishing a goal.

Management process is a process of planning and controlling the performance or execution of any type of activity.

Management science (MS), is the discipline of using mathematical modeling and other analytical methods, to help make better business management decisions.

Megaproject is an extremely large-scale investment project.

Motivation is the set of reasons that prompts one to engage in a particular behavior.

N

Nonlinear Management (NLM) is a superset of management techniques and strategies that allows order to emerge by giving organizations the space to self-organize, evolve and adapt, encompassing Agile, Evolutionary and Lean approaches, as well as many others.

O

Operations management is an area of business that is concerned with the production of good quality goods and services, and involves the responsibility of ensuring that business operations are efficient and effective. It is the management of resources, the distribution of goods and services to customers, and the analysis of queue systems.

Operations, see **Business operations**

Operations Research (OR) is an interdisciplinary branch of applied mathematics and formal science that uses methods such as mathematical modeling, statistics, and algorithms to arrive at optimal or near optimal solutions to complex problems.

Organization is a social arrangement which pursues collective goals, which controls its own performance, and which has a boundary separating it from its environment.

Organization development (OD) is a planned, structured, organization-wide effort to increase the organization's effectiveness and health.

P

Planning in organizations and public policy is both the organizational process of creating and maintaining a plan; and the psychological process of thinking about the activities required to create a desired goal on some scale.

Portfolio in finance is an appropriate mix of or collection of investments held by an institution or a private individual.

PRINCE2 : PRINCE2 is a project management methodology. The planning, monitoring and control of all aspects of the project and the motivation of all those involved in it to achieve the project objectives on time and to the specified cost, quality and performance.

Process is an ongoing collection of activities, with an inputs, outputs and the energy required to transform inputs to outputs.

Process architecture is the structural design of general process systems and applies to fields such as computers (software, hardware, networks, etc.), business processes (enterprise architecture, policy and procedures, logistics, project management, etc.), and any other process system of varying degrees of complexity.

Process management is the ensemble of activities of planning and monitoring the performance of a process, especially in the sense of business process, often confused with reengineering.

Product breakdown structure (PBS) in project management is an exhaustive, hierarchical tree structure of components that make up an item, arranged in whole-part relationship.

Product description in project management is a structured format of presenting information about a project product

Program Evaluation and Review Technique (PERT) is a statistical tool, used in project management, designed to analyze and represent the tasks involved in completing a given project.

Program Management is the process of managing multiple ongoing inter-dependent projects. An example would be that of designing, manufacturing and providing support infrastructure for an automobile manufacturer.

Project : A temporary endeavor undertaken to create a unique product, service, or result.

Project accounting Is the practice of creating financial reports specifically designed to track the financial progress of projects, which can then be used by managers to aid project management.

Project Cost Management A method of managing a project in real-time from the estimating stage to project control; through the use of technology cost, schedule and productivity is monitored.

Project management : The complete set of tasks, techniques, tools applied during project execution'.

Project Management Body of Knowledge (PMBOK) : The sum of knowledge within the profession of project management that is standardized by ISO.

Project management office: The Project management office in a business or professional enterprise is the department or group that defines and maintains the standards of process, generally related to project management, within the organization. The PMO strives to standardize and introduce economies of repetition in the execution of projects. The PMO is the source of documentation, guidance and metrics on the practice of project management and execution.

Project management process is the management process of planning and controlling the performance or execution of a project.

Project Management Professional is a certificated professional in project management.

Project Management Simulators are computer-based tools used in project management training programs. Usually, project management simulation is a group exercise. The computer-based simulation is an interactive learning activity.

Project management software is a type of software, including scheduling, cost control and budget management, resource allocation, collaboration software, communication, quality management and documentation or administration systems, which are used to deal with the complexity of large projects.

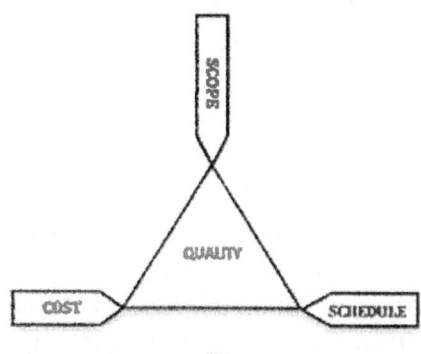

Project Management Triangle

Project Management Triangle is a model of the constraints of project management.

Project manager : professional in the field of project management. Project managers can have the responsibility of the planning, execution, and closing of any project, typically relating to construction industry, architecture, computer networking, telecommunications or software development.

Project network is a graph (flow chart) depicting the sequence in which a project's terminal elements are to be completed by showing terminal elements and their dependencies.

Project plan is a formal, approved document used to guide both *project execution* and *project control*. The primary uses of the project plan are to document planning assumptions and decisions, facilitate communication among *stakeholders*, and document approved scope, cost, and schedule *baselines*. A project plan may be summary or detailed.

Project planning is part of project management, which relates to the use of schedules such as Gantt charts to plan and subsequently report progress within the project environment.

Project stakeholders are those entities within or without an organization which sponsor a project or, have an interest or a gain upon a successful completion of a project.

Project team is the management team leading the project, and provide services to the project. Projects often bring together a variety number of problems. Stakeholders have important issues with others.

Proport refers to the combination of the unique skills of an organisation's members for collective advantage.

Q

Quality can mean a high degree of excellence ("a quality product"), a degree of excellence or the lack of it ("work of average quality"), or a property of something ("the addictive quality of alcohol").[1] Distinct from the vernacular, the subject of this article is the business interpretation of quality.

Quality, Cost, Delivery(QCD) as used in lean manufacturing measures a businesses activity and develops Key performance indicators. QCD analysis often forms a part of continuous improvement programs

R

Reengineering is radical redesign of an organization's processes, especially its business processes. Rather than organizing a firm into functional specialties (like production, accounting, marketing, etc.) and considering the tasks that each function performs; complete processes from materials acquisition, to production, to marketing and distribution should be considered. The firm should be re-engineered into a series of processes.

Resources are what is required to carry out a project's tasks. They can be people, equipment, facilities, funding, or anything else capable of definition (usually other than labour) required for the completion of a project activity.

Risk is the precise probability of specific eventualities.

Risk management is a management specialism aiming to reduce different risks related to a preselected domain to the level accepted by society. It may refer to numerous types of threats caused by environment, technology, humans, organizations and politics.

Risk register is a tool commonly used in project planning and organizational risk assessments.

S

Schedules in project management consists of a list of a project's terminal elements with intended start and finish dates.

Scientific management is a theory of management that analyzes and synthesizes workflow processes, improving labor productivity.

Scope of a project in project management is the sum total of all of its products and their requirements or features.

Scope creep refers to uncontrolled changes in a project's scope. This phenomenon can occur when the scope of a project is not properly defined, documented, or controlled. It is generally considered a negative occurrence that is to be avoided.

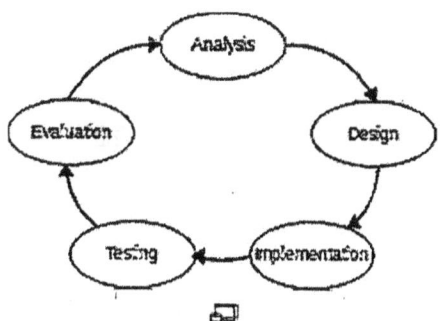

The systems development life cycle.

Scrum is an iterative incremental process of software development commonly used with agile software development. Despite the fact that "Scrum" is not an acronym, some companies implementing the process have been known to adhere to an all capital letter expression of the word, i.e. SCRUM.

Six Sigma is a business management strategy, originally developed by Motorola, that today enjoys widespread application in many sectors of industry.

Software engineering is the application of a systematic, disciplined, quantifiable approach to the development, operation, and maintenance of software.[1]

Systems Development Life Cycle (SDLC) is any logical process used by a systems analyst to develop an information system, including requirements, validation, training, and user ownership. An SDLC should result in a high quality system that meets or exceeds customer expectations, within time and cost estimates, works effectively and efficiently in the current and planned Information Technology infrastructure, and is cheap to maintain and cost-effective to enhance.

Systems engineering is an interdisciplinary field of engineering that focuses on how complex engineering projects should be designed and managed.

T

Task is part of a set of actions which accomplish a job, problem or assignment.

Tasks in project management are activity that needs to be accomplished within a defined period of time.

Task analysis is the analysis or a breakdown of exactly how a task is accomplished, such as what sub-tasks are required

Timeline is a graphical representation of a chronological sequence of events, also referred to as a chronology. It can also mean a schedule of activities, such as a timetable.

U

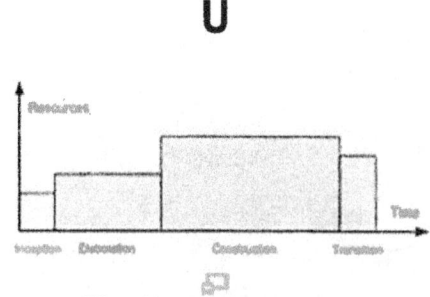

The Unified Process.

Unified Process: The Unified process is a popular iterative and incremental software development process framework. The best-known and extensively documented refinement of the Unified Process is the Rational Unified Process (RUP).

V

Value engineering (VE) is a systematic method to improve the "value" of goods and services by using an examination of function. Value, as defined, is the ratio of function to cost. Value can therefore be increased by either improving the function or reducing the cost. It is a primary tenet of value engineering that basic functions be preserved and not be reduced as a consequence of pursuing value improvements.

Vertical slice is a type of milestone, benchmark, or deadline, with emphasis on demonstrating progress across all components of a project.

Virtual Design and Construction (VDC) is the use of integrated multi-disciplinary performance models of design-construction projects, including the Product (i.e., facilities), Work Processes and Organization of the design - construction - operation team in order to support explicit and public business objectives.

W

Wideband Delphi is a consensus-based estimation technique for estimating effort.

Work in project management is the amount of effort applied to produce a deliverable or to accomplish a task (a terminal element).

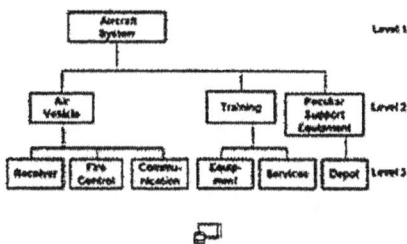
A work breakdown structure.

Work Breakdown Structure (WBS) is a tool that defines a project and groups the project's discrete work elements in a way that helps organize and define the total work scope of the project. A Work breakdown structure element may be a product, data, a service, or any combination. WBS also provides the necessary framework for detailed cost estimating and control along with providing guidance for schedule development and control.

Work package is a subset of a project that can be assigned to a specific party for execution. Because of the similarity, work packages are often misidentified as projects.

Workstream is a set of associated activities, focused around a particular scope that follow a path from initiation to completion.